Praise for *A School Leader's Guide to Understanding Attitudes and Influencing Behavior*

In this book, Brandt and Caroline Pryor have presented us with ideas and techniques that will assist the average administrator in successfully addressing needed improvements. It is my intention to add important concepts presented in this book to my principal and superintendent preparation courses.

Elvis H. Arterbury
Professor of Educational Leadership
Lamar University, Texas

Given the press for school administrators to implement and manage change, this book provides a framework for identifying why new initiatives are resisted and how best to reduce or eliminate this resistance. Teachers also will find the book to be useful in understanding why students possess certain attitudes and how these can be altered. The authors' ideas are quite easy to follow because of the clear description of terms, readable figures and tables, and ample numbers of examples and cases to illustrate how the model works in practice.

Bruce Barnett, Professor
University of Texas at San Antonio

Education is a 'people' business; the most successful school leaders are those who have a full understanding of the individuals and groups they lead. This book provides a practical framework that enables school leaders to effectively assess the attitudes and better understand the behaviors of their staff. It is a tool that will help leaders make sense of the complexities of human and group dynamics, empowering them to make informed decisions. Schools are in need of strong leadership, and this book provides an important building block for great leaders.

Kevin Brown, Director of Personnel
Alamo Heights Independent School District, Texas

As a former public school administrator for many years, and now at the university level, I believe principals will find important topics that are thought provoking and in turn applicable. An excellent tool for administrators.

Larry Butler
Coordinator, Middle Grades Program
Texas A&M University

This book is a valuable tool for strengthening the principal's ability to systematically move a school in an educationally productive direction. This book would be extremely valuable as part of a principal preparation program. It gives principals an effective leadership strategy that they can integrate and personalize in their schools. At the same time, it is highly readable and very direct in its presentation, enabling individuals or small groups of school leaders to make significant, positive changes in the way their school operates.

David A. Erlandson, Professor
Texas A&M University

Brandt and Caroline Pryor's new book fills a major void in the literature focused upon Educational Leadership. This volume takes readers from the theoretical concepts of implementing change to practical applications. It is a must-have resource for those leaders who are instituting change in their work place and an excellent resource for students in Educational Leadership programs.

Robert J. Fallows, Associate Professor
Northern Arizona University

School administrators, as well as leaders in a variety of organizational settings, will find this book a valuable tool in their arsenal of strategies to run effective, efficient, flexible organizations. While the book is aimed at leaders in education, the examples and techniques are applicable to a wide variety of individuals in leadership positions. I would recommend this book to those interested in organizational change, personnel development, public policy, and effective leadership strategies across sectors. The book is well written providing the concepts, tools, and techniques necessary for immediate application.

James F. Gilsinan, Dean
St. Louis University, Missouri

Today's principals are in the hot seat. This book will help principals understand how to approach problem solving and decision making for successful outcomes.

Cordell T. Jones, Principal
Woodridge Elementary, Texas

Successful school leaders are not only instructional leaders, they are also opinion leaders who set the tone and direction for schools. This book can help principals or other administrators by placing the research on attitudes and a model for understanding them into a school context. It provides a process that school leaders can follow when trying to influence people's attitudes.

Joe O'Reilly
Director of Research and Planning
Mesa Public Schools, Texas

Brandt and Carolyn Pryor have done an exceptional job of blending theory and practice. Written for the school administrator, this book is clear, concise and useful. It provides a tool that can bring about change and positively impact student performance and achievement.

Fred H. Richardson
Manager, High School Redesign
Communities Foundation of Texas

Educational administrators will find the book to be an easily applicable tool for solving many of the dilemmas they face in their schools.

Theron Schutte, Principal
Boone Middle School, Iowa

This book is a welcome addition to the knowledge base on school leadership and is an excellent text for preparing preservice school leaders in courses on the psychology of leadership. Beyond providing a useful framework to examine behavioral changes in schools, this book delves into the details of how attitudinal change occurs and provides the reader with a process for transforming behavioral changes in schools. It is a highly practitioner-friendly book that school leaders and professional development planners will find useful.

Alan R. Shoho
Associate Professor
University of Texas

Finally a book that can serve as a useful tool for aspiring and practicing school leaders. Today's school leader needs strategies and competencies in working with diverse audience and perspectives. This book will be a great resource to the school leader who realizes the importance of using data in everyday decision making. This step-by-step guide to changing attitudes and influencing behavior is essential reading in this age of accountability.

Luana Zellner
Director, The Principals' Center
Texas A&M University

THE SCHOOL LEADER'S GUIDE TO UNDERSTANDING ATTITUDE AND INFLUENCING BEHAVIOR

WORKING WITH TEACHERS, PARENTS, STUDENTS, AND THE COMMUNITY

BRANDT W. PRYOR   **CAROLINE R. PRYOR**

CORWIN PRESS
A Sage Publications Company
Thousand Oaks, California

For information:

Corwin Press
A Sage Publications Company
2455 Teller Road
Thousand Oaks, California 91320
www.corwinpress.com

Sage Publications Ltd.
1 Oliver's Yard
55 City Road
London EC1Y 1SP
United Kingdom

Sage Publications India Pvt. Ltd.
B-42, Panchsheel Enclave
Post Box 4109
New Delhi 110 017 India

Printed in the United States of America

Library of Congress Cataloging-in-Publication Data

Pryor, Brandt.
The school leader's guide to understanding attitude and influencing behavior: Working with teachers, parents, students, and the community / Brandt W. and Caroline R. Pryor.
    p. cm.
Includes bibliographical references and index.
ISBN 1-4129-0445-5 (cloth) - ISBN 1-4129-0446-3 (pbk.)
    1. School management and organization. 2. Educational leadership. 3. Attitude change. I. Pryor, Caroline R. II. Title.
LB2805.P924 2005   2004018168

This book is printed on acid-free paper.

04   05   06   10   9   8   7   6   5   4   3   2   1

Acquisitions Editor:	Rachel Livsey
Editorial Assistant:	Phyllis Cappello
Production Editor:	Diane S. Foster
Copy Editor:	Mark Newton, Publication Services
Typesetter:	C&M Digitals (P) Ltd.
Proofreader:	Cheryl Rivard
Indexer:	Karen McKenzie
Cover Designer:	Michael Dubowe

Contents

Preface   ix

Acknowledgements   xiii

About the Authors   xv

Part I: A Useful Model for Changing School Behavior   1

1. How Are Attitudes and Behaviors Formed?   3

2. How Are Attitudes Toward
   People Formed and Changed?   21

3. How Are Attitudes Toward
   Behaviors Formed and Changed?   35

4. How Is Perceived Social
   Pressure Formed and Changed?   45

5. Putting It All Together: The Model as a Whole   55

Part II: Conducting Your Study   61

6. Narrowing Your Interest   63

7. Collecting Your Data   69

Part III: Understanding and Applying Your Results   83

8. Analyzing and Reporting Your Results   85

9. Applying Your Results to Your Interest   99

Resource A: Glossary of Key Terms   111

Resource B: Sample Scales   113

Resource C: Sample Questionnaire   117

Resource D: Action Plan Checklist
for a Study Using the Model   127

Resource E: Internet-Based Resources   131

References   133

Index   137

List of Figures

Figure 1.1 Formation of Intention by Attitude and Norm — 4
Figure 2.1 Formation of Attitude Toward an Object — 25
Figure 3.1 Formation of Attitude Toward a Behavior — 39
Figure 4.1 Formation of Social Pressure Regarding a Behavior — 49
Figure 5.1 The Model of Reasoned Action — 56
Figure 8.1 Hypothetical Results From
Applying the Model of Reasoned Action — 97

List of Tables

Table 2.1 Formation of Mrs. Thompson's
Attitude Toward the School (*Before* Intervention) — 29
Table 2.2 Change of Mrs. Thompson's
Attitude Toward the School (*After* Intervention) — 31
Table 3.1 Formation of Mrs. Thompson's
Attitude Toward Resigning (*Before* Intervention) — 40
Table 3.2 Change of Mrs. Thompson's
Attitude Toward Resigning (*After* Intervention) — 42
Table 4.1 Formation of Mrs. Thompson's
Subjective Norm (*Before* Intervention) — 51
Table 4.2 Change of Mrs. Thompson's
Subjective Norm (*After* Intervention) — 52
Table 7.1 Organization of Salient Beliefs
About Outcomes of Resigning From Teaching — 74
Table 7.2 Identification of Common Salient Outcome Beliefs — 76
Table 8.1 Facsimile of SPSS Frequency
Distribution of Scores on Intention — 90
Table 8.2 Differences in Mean Scores of
High- and Low-Intention Groups — 93
Table 8.3 Differences in Scores on Outcome
Beliefs, Evaluations, and Products by Intention Group — 94
Table 8.4 Differences in Scores on Normative
Beliefs, Motivations, and Products by Intention Group — 95
Table 9.1 Differences in Scores on Outcome
Beliefs, Evaluations, and Products by Intention Group — 101
Table 9.2 Differences in Scores on Normative Beliefs,
Motivations, and Products by Intention Group — 107

Preface

We have written this book to bring a highly useful model to school leaders at the building, district, and state levels. Use of the model of reasoned action (MORA) can enhance decision making, problem solving, and planning. The solving of school problems and the making of policy decisions often require that we anticipate how people will feel about an issue or how they will behave. Often, we want to go further and *influence* how people feel or behave, and the MORA described in this book makes this possible.

This book enables readers to understand how people form attitudes and make decisions about performing—or not performing—a wide variety of future behaviors. These behaviors include voters supporting a school bond issue, teachers integrating technology into their instruction, students staying in school to graduate, and parents monitoring their children's homework. Understanding *why* people feel the way they do about a given issue (e.g., a closed high school campus at lunchtime) can be useful in the making of school policy.

The model of reasoned action (MORA) is based on the assumptions that most people are usually rational, and that they use the information they have in making decisions. People make decisions about their future behavior based on information about the likely consequences of performing the behavior. The model is not intended to explain totally spontaneous, unplanned, or irrational behavior. Many of the more important behaviors, however—the ones that are critical to school success—are planned, however casually, and can be understood by using the MORA.

THE ORIGINS OF THE MODEL
OF REASONED ACTION (MORA)

Social psychologists have investigated the concept of attitude and its relationship to behavior since at least the 1930s. Martin Fishbein (e.g., 1963, 1967) and his colleague (e.g., Fishbein & Ajzen, 1975) clarified and integrated this work, producing the MORA described in this book. This model has been used since the 1960s to study such diverse behaviors as smoking cigarettes (e.g., Fishbein, 1982), voting in an election (e.g., Shepard, 1987), and using public transportation (e.g., Bamberg & Schmidt, 2001, 2003). The model has been called by a variety of names ("Fishbein's model," "a theory of reasoned action," and "the theory of planned behavior").

ORIGINS OF THIS BOOK

The MORA is typically taught only in graduate courses in social psychology. Only in the past decade or so has it begun to be applied to studies of educational decision making (e.g., Pryor, 1990; Thornburg & Pryor, 1998; Ballone & Czerniak, 2001; Kim, 2003). For all practical purposes, therefore, until this book, the MORA was not readily available to school leaders.

Ever since I (Brandt W. Pryor) studied with Dr. Fishbein and two of his postdoctoral fellows, I have been excited about the MORA and eager to share it with others. After a colleague asked if I had written anything on how to apply the MORA, I decided to test interest in it among educators. I developed the workshop *Have You Got "Attitude"?: Measuring, Understanding, and Changing Attitude and Behavior.* The interest shown at the first workshop presentation prompted presentations at three other state and regional meetings and at three national meetings since 1998. That workshop laid the foundation for this volume.

Based on my (Caroline R. Pryor) 25 years of experience in schools, I saw the utility the MORA has for school leaders and asked the first author to lecture to my classes on the model. After seeing the interest with which school leaders in my classes have received it, I suggested focusing this book on them.

WHAT THIS BOOK IS NOT, AND WHAT IT IS

This book is *not* a laundry list of answers to the problems school leaders face every day. Books of that type become outdated very quickly, and more important, "all-purpose" solutions really do not exist. A solution that works with one district, school, or classroom will not necessarily work in all others. This book is *also* not a list of lessons drawn from the experience of a long-practiced administrator. Such volumes (e.g., Barth, 2003) can be quite helpful but are necessarily limited by the author's experiences, perspectives, and limitations.

This book *is* an introduction, and a guide, to a problem-solving technique that can be applied in *many* settings, to solve *specific* problems. This technique draws on theoretical developments and has had nearly four decades of testing and refinement by hundreds of scholars.

This book will help you learn how to understand the attitudes other people form and how to influence them in the desired direction. You might want to know why teachers oppose a particular instructional innovation or why community members support a new campus policy.

Perhaps even more important, this book will show you how to understand the decisions people make to perform—or not perform—certain behaviors, and how to influence those behavioral decisions in the desired direction. This technique for understanding attitudes and behaviors will prove an invaluable tool in the school leader's tool kit.

USE OF THIS BOOK

The book presents this widely tested model in an easy-to-read format. Readers are challenged to apply what they learn as they progress through the book. Planning forms that illustrate the key steps in applying the MORA offer a useful guide, and a variety of other useful materials are found in the Resources section.

Individual readers will benefit from reading this book. As is true of most books, it is likely to be even more beneficial when read in an independent study group, a professional development program, or a graduate course. (Instructors may contact the first author for a course syllabus.) Readers need not be concerned about their level of statistical knowledge as only two analytic statistics are required, and they are described in everyday language. Regardless of your context for reading the book, you will benefit from keeping in mind a situation in which you would like to understand people's attitudes or behavioral intentions. As you read each chapter of the book, think about how you will apply it to your situation.

There isn't always the time *or* the need to *fully* apply the MORA in every situation. For the most important opportunities or problems, however, when you *must* know how best to influence the attitudes or behaviors of others, this book will tell you how. In less critical situations, the understanding of attitudes and behaviors you gain from this book will be useful.

Regardless, this is a tool you can use the rest of your working life. Start now with this practical book, and make a positive difference in attitude in your school or district!

Acknowledgments

W e are most appreciative of the many useful suggestions we received from teachers, principals, and other school leaders who were kind enough to review our book in various drafts. These are:

- Blake Allen, Executive Principal, Stephen F. Austin Middle School, Bryan Independent School District, Bryan, TX
- Mary Bandy, Assistant Principal, Heritage Elementary School, Southside Independent School District, San Antonio, TX
- Kevin Brown, Director of Personnel and Public Information, Alamo Heights Independent School District, San Antonio, TX
- Debbie Diss, Department Head, Business & Technology Department, Chamberlain High School, Tampa, FL
- Jan E. Haney, Program Coordinator, North East Education Center, North East Independent School District, San Antonio, TX
- Cordell Jones, Assistant Principal, Alamo Heights High School, San Antonio, TX
- Scott Sheppard, Principal, Kirbyville Junior High, Kirbyville, TX

We are also most appreciative of the many useful suggestions we received from the practitioners and scholars who reviewed our book, in various drafts, for Corwin Press.

We gratefully acknowledge the hard work, patience and expert guidance of our terrific editorial team at Corwin Press: Rachel Livsey, acquisitions editor; Phyllis Cappello, editorial assistant; Diane Foster, production editor; and Mark Newton, copy editor.

Thank you for your vision and belief in seeing this book through production.

The contributions of the following reviewers are gratefully acknowledged:

Leonard O. Pellicer, Dean
College of Education
    and Organizational
    Leadership
University of La Verne
La Verne, CA

Elaine L. Wilmore, Ph.D.
Dallas Baptist University
Dorothy M. Bush College
    of Education
Professor and Director
Masters in Education
    Programs
Dallas, TX

Dr. Roberta Glaser
Assistant Superintendent
St. Johns Public Schools
St. Johns, MI

Delores B. Lindsey
Assistant Professor
California State University,
    San Marcos
San Marcos, CA

Dr. Rose Weiss
Adjunct Professor
Nova Southeastern
    University
Davie, FL

Dr. Becky J. Cooke
Principal
Evergreen Elementary School
Mead School District
Spokane, WA

Susan N. Imamura
Principal
Manoa Elementary
    School
Honolulu, HI

Theron J. Schutte, Ph.D.
Educational
    Administration
Middle School Principal
Boone Community
    School District
Boone, IA

Dr. Susan Stone Kessler
Assistant Principal
Hillsboro High School
Metropolitan Nashville
    Public Schools
Nashville, TN

About the Authors

 **Brandt W. Pryor** is Director of The Evaluation Group, College of Education, at Texas A&M University, College Station, where he now leads statewide studies of high school reform efforts. He is also an educational research consultant specializing in attitude and behavior studies. He has previously served as Associate Professor, Department of Educational Leadership, Lamar University, and Senior Research Associate in the College of Education at Arizona State University.

He did his doctoral work at the University of Illinois, Urbana-Champaign, where he studied attitude theory and measurement with Martin Fishbein, the world's leading social psychologist. (Dr. Fishbein is now the Harry C. Coles, Jr., Distinguished Professor at the University of Pennsylvania.)

His dissertation research, on which committee Fishbein served, was the first successful application of Fishbein's model to decision making about participation in voluntary educational programs. He later replicated that study in investigations of decision making by schoolteachers, principals, and others. His most recently completed attitude study investigated the participation of information scientists in professional development, and was published in the

Journal of Education in Library and Information Science, 39, 118–133. He is currently studying decisions of teachers and administrators to use interactive video conferencing for professional development, and decisions of teachers to integrate technology into their instruction.

He has spoken on attitudes and behavior since 1984, with high school students, community college teachers, as well as with public school and university teachers, researchers, and administrators. He has presented numerous scholarly papers concerning attitude theory, and has conducted his workshop *Have You Got "Attitude"?: Measuring, Understanding, and Changing Attitude and Behavior* at state and national meetings since 1998.

 **Caroline R. Pryor** is Assistant Professor and Regents Fellow in the Department of Teaching, Learning and Culture, at Texas A&M University, College Station. In 2003 she was selected as a Wye Fellow of The Aspen Institute <http://www.aspeninstitute.org/index.asp>.

She holds a doctorate in Secondary Education from Arizona State University. Her postdoctoral work at Arizona State University concerned the development of a citywide field-based preservice teacher education program, including staff development for principals and mentor teachers. She holds teaching credentials in grades K–9, is a former elementary school teacher, and was the director of an English as a Second Language program.

Her books include *Philosophy of Education Workbook: Writing a Statement of Beliefs and Practices* (2002), *Democratic Practice Workbook: Activities for the Field Experience* (2000), and *Writing a Philosophy Statement: An Educator's Workbook* (2004), all published by McGraw-Hill; as well as *The Mission of the Scholar: Research and Perspectives,* published by Peter Lang (2002).

Currently, her research focuses on democratic classroom discourse strategies, and applying the model to study preservice and mentor teachers' intentions to implement democratic practice. She has also applied aspects of the model in grant project evaluations (e.g., Pryor & Kang, 2003).

She teaches graduate courses in curriculum theory and development. In a career that spans 25 years of teaching, she has worked extensively with principals and teachers in field-based, preservice programs building alliances for school reform.

PART I

A Useful Model for Changing School Behavior

How Are Attitudes and Behaviors Formed?

How Do People Make Decisions About Their Behavior?

Have you ever wished you could look inside the minds of people, to see why they behave as they do, or why they take a certain stand on an issue? Thanks to the model of reasoned action (MORA) described in this book, it is now possible for school leaders to scientifically understand the belief structures that underlie the attitudes and behaviors of diverse constituencies both inside and outside the school.

This understanding offers *two powerful implications* for school leaders. The *first* is that people sometimes hold beliefs that are demonstrably untrue. In such cases, attitudes and behaviors can be influenced by the provision of accurate information. The *second* implication is that

> "... We produce many more qualified teachers than we hire. The hard part is keeping the teachers we prepare."
>
> —Linda Darling-Hammond (2003)

true beliefs suggest possible administrative changes that can influence attitude and behavior in the desired direction.

Two Factors in Behavioral Intention: Attitude and Norm

When we think about the possibility of performing some specific behavior, we make up our minds—form our intentions—based on two factors: a personal factor and a social factor.

- The personal factor is our *attitude* toward performing the behavior.
- The social factor is our *subjective norm,* our perception that those people or groups who are important to us would favor—or oppose—our performing the behavior.

This relationship is illustrated in Figure 1.1.

The norm is *subjective,* because people will often never hear *directly* what their "important others" want them to do, or not do, in a given situation. Instead, they will *infer* the expectations of these persons and groups, based on what they

Figure 1.1   The Formation of Intention by Attitude and Norm

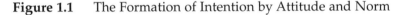

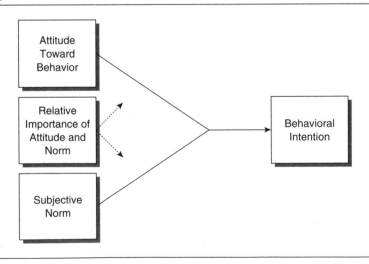

know about each of their "important others" and what they know about the behavior under consideration.

Changing Behavioral Decisions

To change people's behavior, you must change their intentions to perform the behavior. To change intentions, you must change either their attitudes or their norms regarding the behavior (or both). To change attitude or norm, you must change beliefs concerning the behavior.

> "What keeps some people in teaching while others give up?"
>
> —Linda Darling-Hammond (2003)

Relative Importance of Attitude and Norm

Although both factors *can* be important in forming intention, attitude is usually more important. Sometimes, however, subjective norm is the only factor that determines behavioral intention. What accounts for the relative influence of attitudinal and normative influences on intentions?

There is evidence from research to suggest that in behavioral domains in which the decision makers have a lot of information about the behavior (e.g., mandatory testing), attitude is the more important factor. (And when a behavioral domain is important to people, they tend to acquire more information about it.) Sometimes, it is the only significant influence on intention. In domains in which people have *less* information (e.g., technology integration), subjective norm becomes relatively more important.

Research has shown differences in the relative influence of attitude and norm, based on the sex of the decision makers. Personality type might also be important in determining the relative weights. It seems intuitively correct that extroverted people might be relatively *more* influenced by normative considerations than would introverted people.

The relative influence of attitude and norm depends on a number of factors: (a) the decision makers being studied, (b) the behavior of interest, (c) the importance of the behavior to those being studied, and (d) possibly other factors. Research continues to examine these and other possible influences on the relative weights of attitude and norm. The implication is that whenever you are interested in how people are making their decisions about some behavior, the only way to be *sure* about the relative weights of attitude and norm in that specific situation is to study the people and behavior of concern.

The results of my (BWP) first three postdoctoral studies using the MORA suggested to me that respondents who hold positions in their work organizations nearer the top (e.g., assistant superintendent) would be less influenced by norm than those who hold positions further from the top (e.g., teacher's aide). The following year when I began to study school principals' and teachers' decisions about participating in staff development, I assumed that the teachers' decisions would be more influenced by norm than the principals' decisions. The results of those studies, however, surprised me.

> "Keeping good teachers should be one of the most important agenda items for any school leader."
>
> —Linda Darling-Hammond (2003)

The studies found that norm was important for decision making in both groups but that it was *more* important for principals than for teachers. When I reported this finding—and my puzzlement over it—to my client's board of directors, a teacher on that board explained: "That's easy! Being a principal is a very political job!"

BELIEFS ARE THE BASIS OF ATTITUDE AND BEHAVIOR

The model of reasoned action (MORA) states that planned behaviors are ultimately determined by the beliefs that people hold. As both attitude and norm are formed by beliefs, a few words about them will be helpful here. You will find more in-depth explanations of how beliefs form attitude and norm in the next three chapters.

THREE KINDS OF BELIEFS

The *first kind* of belief is a thought that links an object (or person) with a characteristic or quality. For example, a ball might be perfectly round, colored orange, and made of rubber. If you held such a ball in your hand, you would form very strong beliefs that it was round, orange, and rubber. The ball might also be large, with a pebbled surface, and used for playing basketball. It might have Michael Jordan's signature on it. You would probably believe it to be extremely likely that the ball was round, orange, and a basketball, but think it only slightly likely—or maybe *quite un*likely—that the signature is *really* Michael Jordan's! Our beliefs that an object has certain qualities, and our corresponding evaluations of these qualities, form our attitudes toward the object.

The *second kind* of belief is a thought that links your performing some behavior, such as setting a no-homework-on-Friday policy, with likely consequences or outcomes of that behavior. In the case of setting the policy, some appreciation from students and more parental support might be among the likely outcomes you would think of. These beliefs about behavioral outcomes and the corresponding evaluations of the outcomes form our attitudes toward performing behaviors.

The *third kind* of belief is a thought that links your performing some behavior, with the approval, or disapproval, of people who are important to you. These beliefs, and our willingness to comply with each of these "important others," form subjective norm, our perception of social pressure to perform (or not perform) a behavior.

> "... Attrition from individual schools and districts ... particularly affect schools that serve poor and minority students."
>
> —Linda Darling-Hammond (2003)

ACQUIRING BELIEFS

We acquire beliefs in three ways. The *first way* is through *direct observation*. When you first enter a school that is new to you, you will immediately notice a number of qualities about the school. The campus is either attractive and well kept, or it is not. The building is very new, very old, or somewhere in between. You automatically form beliefs that the school has the qualities you observed.

The *second way* we acquire beliefs is by *acceptance of information* from some source such as another person, radio or television, or a written report. If you had heard from someone before your visit that the school is well run and highly successful, you might have believed this information very strongly, only somewhat strongly, or not at all.

The *third way* we acquire beliefs is *by inferring new beliefs* from what we already know. For example, suppose that you believed the information that the school is well run and highly successful. However, when you arrive at the campus, you observe that the grounds and building are quite poorly maintained. From these two beliefs, you might infer that the district lacks the funds for proper maintenance.

RELATIVE IMPORTANCE OF BELIEFS

If, later that same day, you were asked what you thought about the school, you would immediately come up with a small number of beliefs, perhaps five to nine. However, if you concentrated, you could think of many, many more beliefs about the school based on your visit, perhaps 20 or more.

Not all of these beliefs have the same importance, however, in influencing your attitudes and behavior. Since we can keep only a few beliefs (typically five to nine) uppermost in our minds at one time, only those beliefs are important. Those five to nine beliefs are called *salient*, because they *stick out,* from all the other beliefs we have, like the bristles from a hairbrush. (Increasingly, salient beliefs are called "accessible beliefs.")

How Does the Model Extend Previous Ideas in Educational Leadership?

School Culture

The concept of school culture is a powerful one in the literature of educational leadership. Definitions of school culture include such factors as (a) the values and beliefs that determine behavioral norms (Kowalski, 2003), and (b) norms, values, and beliefs (Peterson, 2002).

There is evidence from research that positive school culture is related to such positive qualities as higher teacher morale (e.g., Black, 2001), higher student achievement (e.g., Bruner & Greenlee, 2000), and more successful implementation of reform (e.g., D'Amico & Nelson, 2000). There is evidence that this relationship is causal: Positive changes in culture have been followed by positive changes in student achievement (e.g., Thacker & McInerney, 1992).

Kent Peterson (2002) noted, "Being able to understand and shape the culture is key to a school's success . . ." (p. 10). He suggested that school leaders transform school cultures in three steps: reading, assessing, and shaping the culture. School leaders shape the culture by reinforcing positive aspects of the culture and working to change negative aspects.

The *model of reasoned action* (MORA) presented in this book can *extend* traditional approaches to reading and assessing a school culture by providing more specific information about the beliefs, values, and norms held by various groups in a school, community, or district. The MORA can assess both the strength and direction of the unique sets of beliefs and values held by teachers, students, parents, or other groups.

School Change

Thompson (2001) noted that current challenges to education require that "Principals must, above all, become expert at leading change . . . [and] be skilled at dealing with resistance to change" (p. 2). This requirement applies to school leaders at other levels as well. Resistance to change can come from groups within the school, as well as from groups outside the school.

Teacher Attitudes

The Concerns-Based Adoption Model (CBAM) (Hall & Hord, 2001; Hord et al., 1987) was developed to monitor and increase the adoption of educational innovations. The instrument measures concerns that educators hold when faced with change. Data collected with the instrument are used to indicate which stage of adoption of the innovation a group currently occupies.

A review of the research literature on change (Waugh & Punch, 1987) identified five factors related to teachers' receptivity to change: (a) basic attitudes toward education, (b) resolution of fears about the change, (c) personal cost appraisal for change, (d) practicality of the change, and (e) perceived school support for the change. Welch (1989) asserts that in responding to a proposed change, teachers assess the advantages and disadvantages for them *personally*, not just those for student growth.

The MORA explained in this book extends CBAM by helping you to understand the beliefs and evaluations of a *specific* group (e.g., at the grade, school, or district level) that most strongly contribute to resistance to a *specific* planned change. This information tells what actions or information are most likely to reduce resistance by changing attitudes and behavior in the desired direction. The MORA takes into account all of Waugh and Punch's five factors, as well as the advantages and disadvantages calculation mentioned by Welch.

Student Attitudes

Michael Fullan (2001) reminds us of the importance of students in planning any educational change that requires them to do something new. Their failure to perform as desired can doom the change effort.

The MORA can be used to understand student attitudes toward a change effort, toward a new policy, or toward staying in school to graduate. Application of the MORA can tell you exactly what administrative actions or information provision will be most likely to influence student attitude and behavior in the desired direction.

Community Attitudes

John Goodlad (2004) reminds us of the importance of constituencies outside the school when considering change. School boards, parents, and taxpayers in general can be supportive, indifferent, or hostile to change efforts and must be considered during planning.

The MORA helps you to understand the beliefs and evaluations of a specific group that most strongly contribute to resistance to a specific planned change. This information tells exactly what actions or information are most likely to reduce resistance by changing attitudes and behavior in the desired direction.

Is This the Right Change to Adopt Now?

Administrators in education (especially at the upper levels) generally favor change, but is all change good? Constant change, particularly when the benefits are not immediately apparent, can have a negative effect on the attitudes toward change held by administrators, teachers, and students. All changes are not likely to be concurrently (a) useful, (b) appropriate for the time and setting, and (c) sufficiently supported by those who will actually have to implement the innovation. Sometimes, a given innovation is just not the right thing to do.

Shirley Hord and her colleagues (Hord et al., 1987) argued that it is critical to understand the points of view of those involved in a change effort.

Administrators will benefit from knowing not only *how* key constituencies feel about an impending change but *why* they feel the way they do, that is, which beliefs and evaluations formed their attitudes. Given the current emphasis on "data-driven decision making" (e.g., LaFee, 2002), such an in-depth understanding is especially important.

It is likely that good leaders know how their key constituencies feel about important issues. Until they use the MORA, however, those leaders will not know how those attitudes were formed. They will not know *specifically* what they have to do or what information they have to provide to change attitudes or behavior in the desired direction. Use of the MORA in a diagnostic way—in advance of initiating change—will tell school leaders what they need to know to make the best decisions about change efforts.

Force Field Analysis

Kurt Lewin's (1951) "force field analysis" is a widely used planning tool in business, industry, and education. It was developed for use in diagnosing situations and considering all the important factors. Typically used for planning change, it offers a holistic view of all the forces either for (*driving forces*) or against (*restraining forces*) a plan of change. This "big picture" approach aids thinking of ways to strengthen the driving forces and reduce the impact of the restraining forces.

The lists of driving forces and restraining forces are typically developed by brainstorming, either individually or in a group. (A sufficiently diverse group is more likely to list all of the most important factors that need to be considered.) Some practitioners assign scores to each of the forces based on their estimates of its strength. Other practitioners add a second dimension and include in the score a measure of their estimates of the likelihood that the force can be changed (e.g., either strengthened or weakened). The benefits of this technique are clear, and this is a good starting point. The limitation is that these *estimates* of driving and restraining forces and their relative strengths are typically not based directly on empirical evidence.

The MORA has a sharper focus than force field analysis and extends it by offering leaders a way to measure how opposed a group is to a given plan.

Even more useful for *changing* the opposition, MORA tells the user exactly what information and actions are likely to be most effective in reducing opposition. Neutral groups and groups who are in favor can also be studied to determine how to increase their support for the plan.

FREQUENTLY ASKED QUESTIONS ON USING THE MODEL

When Is the Model Useful, and When Is It Not?

The model is useful for understanding the attitudes and behavioral decisions of groups. However, the understanding it provides regarding how people form attitudes and how people make decisions might serve as a guide in dealing with individuals.

For example, when you encounter someone whose position on a policy you simply don't understand, you might ask what the person sees as the advantages and disadvantages of the policy. This could give you a rough idea of how that person's attitude toward the policy was formed.

USING MORA CONCEPTS
WITHOUT CONDUCTING A STUDY

- What if I do not have the *time or resources* to use the full MORA?
- What if I want to *use MORA for one just person,* not a group of people?
- Can I use MORA for a *quick but limited understanding of beliefs?*

Interview Tip

- Interview the parents, students, teachers, principals, etc.
- Ask questions that will lead to the identification of beliefs such as:

   What are the advantages of _____?

   What are the disadvantages of _____?

Evaluation Tip

- Ask them to tell you the likelihood of each of the advantages (belief strength).
- Ask them to tell you the likelihood of each of the *dis*advantages (belief strength).
- Ask them how bad (negatively evaluated) or good (favorably evaluated) each advantage and disadvantage is.
- Multiply the strength of each belief by its evaluation and sum the scores.

IN WHAT WAYS CAN
THE MODEL BE USEFUL?

Teachers can use the model in a variety of ways. One would be as a form of needs assessment at the beginning of a course. You could ask students what they like and what they dislike about the course. This should give you a general idea of why their attitudes are favorable or unfavorable. It might also suggest ways to make the course more attractive to these students.

Teachers can also use the model to teach about decision making. Take the example of an advanced placement U.S. History (1600–1865) class, at the point of teaching about the beginning of the Civil War. The teacher might ask students to research who the decision makers were concerning the firing on Fort Sumter, South Carolina. The teacher might ask students, "Who were the decision makers in the Confederacy?"; "What beliefs did they have about outcomes of their firing on the fort?"; "How did they evaluate those outcomes?"; and "How realistic were their outcome beliefs?" Students might also be asked to research the referents ("important others") who might have exerted pressure on decision makers and what they believed referents wanted them to do.

Building administrators can use the model to see why parents will support or oppose a new school policy (e.g., closed high school campus at lunchtime). Administrators can use the model to see why teachers will or will not adopt a curriculum innovation, such as cooperative learning in mathematics. Administrators can use the model to see why teachers will or will not integrate technology into their instruction.

District administrators can use the model to see why voters will or will not support a new bond issue or why principals oppose or support a new policy on site-based decision making.

EXAMPLES OF POSSIBLE CONCERNS

District Level

- The school district and teachers continue to have contract disputes.
- Testing drives our curriculum and instruction.
- Administrators require teacher accountability, not professional responsibility.
- Our district does not provide for career ladder benefits.
- Our district does not offer paid teacher sabbatical time.
- Our sick leave policy is inadequate.

(Continued)

- Teacher pay is low.
- The amount of paperwork increases every year.

School Level

- The administration at my school believes in drill-kill activities.
- The administration at my school holds all the power.
- Class size is too large.
- Our school facilities are poorly maintained.
- We do not have adequate technology for our students.
- We do not have adequate support for teachers' use of technology.
- Our students are poorly motivated.
- Parents do not help students with homework.
- Parents do not support teacher decisions.
- Student attitudes on this campus are poor.
- The community does not support our school.
- There is no mentoring program for novice teachers.
- There are few resources for teachers—we run out of supplies.
- Our school is not safe.
- The faculty members at this campus are inexperienced.
- The faculty members at this campus lack a spirit of cooperation.
- This campus lacks a consistent and appropriate discipline policy.

Is It Ethical to Use the Model to Influence Behavior?

This is a rational, information-processing model. You can attempt to influence attitudes and behaviors by providing information. If you have a reputation as a credible source, and if you provide information that is believable, people will probably accept what you tell them. If you do *not* have a reputation as a credible source, or if you provide information that is *not* believable, people will probably *not* accept what you tell them.

Emotion Is a Big Part of Decision Making: How Does the Model Take It Into Account?

Our emotional responses to all the aspects of our world are indeed important. They are a summary of all we know and feel about a given object, issue, or behavior. Emotion is part of the model in that it is used to weight beliefs in the formation of attitudes. In this context, emotion is the evaluation of beliefs about qualities that form attitudes toward objects as well as the evaluation of beliefs about outcomes that form attitudes toward behaviors, as illustrated in Chapters 2 and 3.

OK, This Is a Rational, Information-Processing Model: But What About Irrational People?

One of the many benefits of the model is that it demonstrates the importance of the values we hold. Often people with extremely different value systems might appear to be irrational, but once you understand their value systems, then their positions on issues and their behavior appear more rational.

There are, of course, truly irrational people, and most of us behave somewhat irrationally on occasion. Typically, however, the great majority of people who are considering a given issue or behavior will be thinking rationally, and the thinking of a *group* of people is what the model is designed to help us understand.

Examples Used in the Book

To help illustrate the principles in this book we use a variety of examples, especially in the chapters on formation and change of attitude and norm, and in the chapters on data collection and analysis.

Some examples illustrate processes, and these more complex examples are labeled case studies. There are three of these, all of which concern a hypothetical teacher, Mrs. Thompson.

Case Study 1 is about the formation of Mrs. Thompson's unfavorable (negative) attitude toward her school, and how her principal might change that attitude in a favorable (positive) direction.

Case Study 2 is about the formation of Mrs. Thompson's favorable (positive) attitude toward resigning from teaching, and how her principal might change that attitude in an unfavorable (negative) direction, so she is less likely to retire.

Case Study 3 is about the formation of Mrs. Thompson's perception of social pressure (norm) to resign from teaching, and how her principal might change that norm in an unfavorable (negative) direction, so she is less likely to retire.

In these case studies, we use an individual as an example in order to most simply demonstrate the processes of formation and change of attitude and norm. The model, however, is designed to explain the behavioral intentions, attitudes, and norms of a group of people. Therefore, in Chapter 9, we describe use of the model with a group of people.

The costs of teacher attrition to school districts are extremely high and are necessarily a concern to educational leaders. Whether good teachers leave a school, leave a district, or leave teaching entirely, there are a variety of costs.

One is the cost of recruiting, hiring, and orienting new teachers. A second cost is the continuity in curriculum alignment that has been developed. A third is the lost investment in professional development.

Although teacher pay is important, it is not always the most important factor in teacher attrition. Often other beliefs about teaching in the school or district and working with parents or students are the greatest influences on teachers' attitudes toward remaining in a school, a district, or the field. To most effectively reduce teacher attrition, it is essential to understand the *particular beliefs* that underlie the attitudes toward leaving or remaining in a school or district of the *particular* teachers of concern.

Many of the examples in this book, therefore, focus on teacher attrition. There are a variety of other behaviors for which the model will be useful and a variety of other groups (e.g., students, parents, principals) that might be studied using the model.

We use hypothetical data in all these examples in order to illustrate an idea or principle, something that is not always possible with actual data. For example, there are three ways of influencing attitude and norm in the desired direction, but not all *actual* data sets would allow each of these three ways to be used.

Organization of the Book

Part I: A Useful Model for Changing School Behavior

- Chapter 1 introduces the basic concepts of the model of reasoned action (MORA), the formation of beliefs, attitudes, perceptions of social pressure, and behavioral decisions. The chapter shows how the MORA fits with previous thinking in educational leadership, and it also answers frequently asked questions such as those about the utility, practicality, and ethics of using the model.

- Chapters 2 through 4 provide a more detailed explanation, including plenty of examples, of how we form our attitudes toward things, toward performing behaviors, as well as our perceptions of social pressure concerning future behavior.

- Chapter 5 puts all the parts together and helps you see the model as a whole.

Part II: Conducting Your Study

- Chapter 6 helps you refine a situation in your school or community into a resolvable question using the MORA.

- Chapter 7 tells you—step-by-step—how to collect the data.

Part III: Understanding and Applying Your Results

- Chapter 8 tells you how to analyze, understand, and report the results.
- Chapter 9 tells you how to use these results for school improvement.

2

How Are Attitudes Toward People Formed and Changed?

BASIC CONCEPTS

Attitude Defined

The model of reasoned action (MORA) presented in this book defines attitude as a favorable, unfavorable, or neutral feeling toward some object, person, or behavior. In brief, attitudes are the feelings we have about the people and things in our lives. For example, we have feelings about (a) objects, such as the schools in which we work, or people, such as teachers in our school, and (b) behaviors, such as enrolling in a graduate program or reading this book.

Attitudes can vary in both strength and direction. They can range from *extremely favorable* to *extremely unfavorable*, through a neutral midpoint (*neither favorable nor unfavorable*).

Types and Levels of Attitude

There are essentially *two types* of attitude. The *first type* is *attitude toward an object* (or person). We have positive and negative feelings about objects such as our alma mater, the organization where we work, and our hometown. (We also have feelings about individuals such as a member of our family, and groups such as our neighbors or the local PTO.) The *second type* of attitude is an *attitude toward a behavior,* such as parents voting in favor of a school bond issue, or principals registering for professional development. This type of attitude is discussed in Chapter 3.

There are also *two levels* of attitude. The *first level* is a *global attitude,* such as "I like history books." The *second level* is a *specific attitude,* such as "I don't like that book on the history of Venetian glassblowing."

A global attitude toward an object (e.g., professional development) cannot be expected to predict any specific attitude (e.g., a professional development program on mainstreaming students with limited English proficiency). It will, however, indicate a general or overall predisposition.

Formation of Attitude Toward an Object

Beliefs About Qualities of an Object

As we consider an object, such as a standardized test, we automatically begin to think about characteristics or qualities of the object. As mentioned in Chapter 1, we can keep only a limited number of beliefs uppermost in our minds at one time. These five to nine "top-of-the-head" thoughts are known as *salient,* because they *stick out* from all the other ideas we have in the backs of our minds. (Think of mountain peaks sticking out from a plain.) Only the salient beliefs are important in forming attitude toward an object. We will believe it more likely that the object has some of these qualities than it has of others.

We will believe it *extremely likely* that the object has some qualities but only *slightly likely* that it has others. Of course, based on differences in the information they have, different people will have somewhat different sets of beliefs about the qualities of a given object, and not all people will agree on the likelihood of any given quality.

The strength and direction of belief that a given object has a given quality can be measured by the scale shown below. (Although people do not form beliefs that they think are *un*likely, the scale measures likelihood in both directions, so that people who do *not* believe in the likelihood of a quality's being associated with the object can indicate their disbelief.)

extremely likely __:__:__:__:__:__:__ extremely unlikely

Evaluations of Qualities

We not only form beliefs about the likely qualities of an object, but we also automatically make evaluations of each quality based on our own long-term values and our immediate concerns. Our evaluations can range from *extremely good* to *extremely bad* through a neutral midpoint (*neither good nor bad*). The scale shown below can measure the strength and direction of evaluation of a quality.

extremely good __:__:__:__:__:__:__ extremely bad

Both probability and evaluative scales are scored as shown below. These scales are scored from +3 to represent the *extremely likely* or *extremely good* end of the continuum, to –3 to represent the *extremely unlikely* or *extremely bad* end of the continuum through a neutral midpoint of zero (*neither likely nor unlikely, neither good nor bad*).

extremely $\underline{+3} : \underline{+2} : \underline{+1} : \underline{0} : \underline{-1} : \underline{-2} : \underline{-3}$ extremely

Belief-Evaluation Products

The multiplication of the strength of our belief in the likelihood that an object has a given quality, and our evaluation of that quality, results in the belief-evaluation product.

This product determines the direction and strength of that outcome's contribution toward attitude.

For example, if we believe that it is only *slightly likely* (+1) that going to a staff development workshop will help us learn something useful, even though we believe that learning something useful is *extremely good* (+3), the belief-evaluation product will be only +3. This will make only a small, although positive, contribution to our attitude.

If, however, we read a brochure on the workshop that includes testimonials from people we respect, we might believe it to be *quite likely* (+2) that we would learn something at the workshop. This would double the belief-evaluation product (from +3 to +6), and therefore double the positive contribution of that outcome to our attitude toward attending the workshop.

Our beliefs about the qualities of an object and our evaluations of those qualities combine to form attitude toward the object, as shown in Figure 2.1.

Summary

It stands to reason that if we *favorably* evaluate most of the qualities we associate with an object, we are likely to have a favorable attitude toward that object. Conversely, if we *unfavorably* evaluate most of the qualities we associate with an object, we are likely to have an unfavorable attitude toward that object.

For example, a high school teacher whose college-bound students must take the SAT might believe that the test has a number of qualities, including (a) that it is easier than it used to be, but (b) that it still discriminates against some students, and (c) it doesn't measure everything that is important.

Let us assume, for example, that she believes it equally likely that the test has all three qualities. She evaluates the first quality somewhat favorably and the second two qualities very unfavorably. She will have an unfavorable attitude toward the SAT on the basis of these three qualities and her evaluations of them.

Figure 2.1   Formation of Attitude Toward an Object

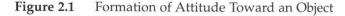

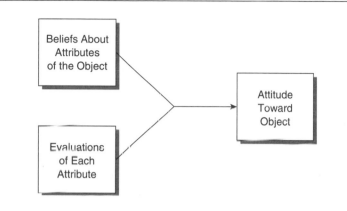

Attitude Change

Once you know how a group of people think and feel about an object—what their attitudes are, and how they are formed (the set of beliefs and evaluations)—you can effectively try to influence those attitudes in the desired direction. This can only be done by providing those people with information that they will believe. There are three ways in which this knowledge of how attitudes are formed can be used to influence attitudes in the desired direction. The example given below illustrates how these three ways can be used.

CASE STUDY 1: FORMATION AND CHANGE OF ATTITUDE TOWARD THE SCHOOL

The two definitions of the concept of *school culture* mentioned in Chapter 1 both included the concept of *beliefs*, and beliefs are the foundation of attitude. It would seem that teachers' beliefs about the qualities (or attributes) of their school would necessarily be an important part of their perception of that school's culture.

Now we will examine how beliefs arise in one teacher's mind and how they determine her attitude toward her school.

The change of attitude and behavior in schools will not always be as easy as portrayed in our examples, as informational messages might not always be believed. Also, depending on the set of beliefs and evaluations, it might not always be possible to employ each of the three ways of change. As would be expected, in some circumstances, change of any degree will be impossible. But more change is likely to be accomplished by the use of this model than by guesswork about what information will be effective in bringing about change.

Although administrators would be more likely to study a group of teachers, parents, or students than an individual, we use just one hypothetical teacher in the examples below. Parts II and III of the book illustrate all the steps of investigating a group of teachers.

Formation of Negative Attitude Toward the School

Background

Jennifer Thompson is a fourth-grade teacher at River Elementary School, a large campus that brings together students from diverse backgrounds and experiences. She is 38 years old, married with two middle school–age children, and has been teaching for eight years, in Grades 3 through 5. This is her second year teaching fourth grade. Mrs. Thompson is an excellent teacher with a good reputation in the school for her technology skills, and is she a leader among teachers in developing innovative curriculum for students.

Mrs. Thompson is thinking about resigning from teaching to pursue a master's degree in computer science full-time, and then seek a job in private industry. She plans to find part-time work while earning her degree. She knows that jobs in private industry can be competitive and will be less secure than teaching. Yet she is attracted to the idea.

What beliefs might she hold that would motivate her to leave her position as a teacher, and what could a principal do to retain her? Let's look first at her attitude toward her school (an *object*), and then, in Chapter 3, her attitude toward resigning from teaching at the school (a *behavior*).

BELIEFS THAT FORM ATTITUDE

Mrs. Thompson believes that her school has a number of qualities that she negatively evaluates. Some of her students are uncooperative, hard to control, and have spotty attendance. Parents don't seem to be involved much in their children's education and are not supportive of the teachers on homework and discipline issues. Mrs. Thompson receives little support from her principal on disciplinary issues, has insufficient resources (e.g., books, computers), and has too many demands on her time (e.g., yard duty, bus duty, hall duty). Finally, in recent years the burden of district-mandated pretesting, curriculum revision, and state-mandated standardized testing has become excessive.

Mrs. Thompson also believes that her school has a number of qualities that she positively evaluates. She likes the noncompetitiveness and the stability of teaching in her school. She likes the fact that she has been able to make a real difference in the lives of some of her students, helping students who were not achieving to become seekers of knowledge who do well after they exit her class. She also likes her fellow teachers and enjoys what interaction her schedule allows with them, whether talking about the curriculum or helping them to create something new in the computer lab.

Table 2.1 reports the strength with which Mrs. Thompson believes that her school has each of these qualities, how she evaluates each quality, and the belief-evaluation products that, together, form her attitude toward the school. Given all the information about her school that she has acquired in eight years of service, it is not surprising that she has nine salient beliefs. Mrs. Thompson's attitude toward her school is –30, which is rather unfavorable.

How Unfavorable Is It?

She has nine salient beliefs about qualities of her school. Each belief could range from +3 (*extremely likely*) to +1 (*slightly likely*). (It is unlikely that a belief that she believed to be *neither likely nor unlikely* [0] would be salient in forming her attitude. If we were looking at a group instead of an individual, this range would extend to +3 to −3, to allow people to express *dis*belief.) Her evaluations of each quality can range from +3 to −3. Given these ranges on beliefs and evaluations, each belief-evaluation product could potentially range from +9 to −9. With nine belief-evaluation products, the summed products (an estimated measure of attitude) could potentially range from +81 to −81.

If *you* were Mrs. Thompson's principal, and you knew the information in Table 2.1, what would you do to influence her attitude in a favorable direction?

Change to Positive Attitude Toward the School

Once you know what qualities someone believes an object possesses and how the person evaluates each quality, you know what information you need to provide to influence the person's attitude in the desired direction. (It works the same way, of course, for influencing a group of people.) There are three ways in which to use this information.

First Way to Change

The first thing Mrs. Thompson's principal could do to influence Mrs. Thompson's attitude toward the school in a *favorable direction* is to *reduce the strength of beliefs that are negatively evaluated,* those that make a negative contribution to attitude. Remember, people can hold *untrue* beliefs.

In the case of her concern about insufficient resources, Mrs. Thompson's principal has just received word that the technology grant proposal she submitted last fall was funded, but she has not yet announced the grant. The school will soon

Table 2.1   Formation of Mrs. Thompson's Attitude Toward the
School (*Before Intervention*)

Quality	Belief	Evaluation	Product
Students uncooperative, hard to control	+1	−3	−3
Little parental support or involvement	+3	−3	−9
Little support from principal on discipline	+3	−3	−9
Too many demands on time	+2	−3	−6
Insufficient resources (books, computers)	+3	−3	−9
Excessive testing	+2	−3	−6
Noncompetitive, stable job	+2	+3	+6
Chance to make real difference in students' lives	+1	+3	+3
Interaction with fellow teachers	+1	+3	+3
		Attitude = −30	

Note: Belief and evaluation scales are scored from +3 (*extremely likely, extremely favorable*) to −3 (*extremely unlikely, extremely unfavorable*) through a neutral midpoint (*neither*) of zero.

be receiving more computers for the computer lab and a laptop computer for each teacher. When Mrs. Thompson learns this, it is likely to considerably reduce the strength of her belief that there are not sufficient resources.

Of course, people can hold true beliefs that are negatively evaluated, and therefore make a negative contribution to attitude. These suggest things that the principal can change. For example, Mrs. Thompson's extremely strong belief that she receives little parental support or involvement combined with her extremely negative evaluation of this quality makes the strongest possible negative contribution to her attitude toward the school.

This information offers an opportunity for the principal to take direct action in developing a schoolwide program to more strongly involve parents in their children's education. Once Mrs. Thompson hears about this program, the strength of her belief will likely be reduced from +3 to perhaps even +1, as shown in Table 2.2. This change in belief strength will reduce that belief-evaluation product from −9 to −3, a marked change.

Another belief that makes the strongest possible negative contribution to her attitude is her concern about the principal's lack of support on discipline. If the principal included Mrs. Thompson on the new school disciplinary committee and promised the committee complete support, the strength of Mrs. Thompson's belief might be largely reduced, from +3 to perhaps even 0, eliminating the belief's negative contribution to her attitude, as shown in Table 2.2.

Second Way to Change

The second thing Mrs. Thompson's principal could do is to *increase the strength of beliefs that are positively evaluated* but are weakly believed, thus increasing the strength of their positive contribution to attitude.

Mrs. Thompson evaluates interaction with her fellow teachers as extremely good (+3), but she doesn't believe strongly that her school offers much interaction. By providing opportunities for more interaction, the principal could increase belief strength from +1 to +2, as shown in Table 2.2. This would double the belief-evaluation product from +3 to +6, dramatically increasing the positive contribution to attitude made by this quality and its evaluation.

For example, the principal might host a fourth-grade team breakfast at school and suggest to them ways in which they might collaborate, such as team teaching or sharing resources (e.g., creating a "fourth-grade book cart").

As can be seen in Table 2.2, these changes so far have markedly changed Mrs. Thompson's attitude from a strongly negative one (−30) to one that is only slightly negative (−6). There is still, however, more that could be done.

Table 2.2   Change of Mrs. Thompson's Attitude Toward the School (*After Intervention*)

Quality	Belief		Evaluation	Product	
Old Beliefs					
Students uncooperative, hard to control	~~+1~~	0	−3	~~−3~~	0
Little parental support or involvement	~~+3~~	+1	−3	~~−9~~	−3
Little support from principal on discipline	~~+3~~	0	−3	~~−9~~	0
Too many demands on time	+2		−3	−6	
Insufficient resources (books, computers)	~~+3~~	+1	−3	~~−9~~	−3
Excessive testing	+2		−3	−6	
Non-competitive, stable job	+2		+3	+6	
Chance to make real difference in students	~~+1~~	0	+3	~~+3~~	0
Interaction with fellow teachers	~~+1~~	+2	+3	~~+3~~	+6
			Old Attitude =	~~30~~	−6
New Beliefs					
I make a real difference in the lives of my fellow teachers	+2		+3	+6	
Can lay foundation for career improvement	+3		+3	+9	
			New Beliefs =	+15	
			New Attitude =	+9	

Note: Belief and evaluation scales are scored from +3 (*extremely likely, extremely favorable*) to −3 (*extremely unlikely, extremely unfavorable*) through a neutral midpoint (*neither*) of zero. Beliefs that are italicized have lost their salience and are no longer an influence on attitude.

Third Way to Change

The third thing Mrs. Thompson's principal could do is to provide information that would *add new beliefs* about school qualities that Mrs. Thompson would positively evaluate.

For example, note her highly positive evaluations of the two qualities (a) "Interaction with fellow teachers" and (b) "Chance to make a difference in students' lives."

Given these evaluations, Mrs. Thompson is also likely to positively evaluate the belief "I make a real difference in the lives of my fellow teachers." If the principal informed Mrs. Thompson's fellow teachers of her impending resignation and encouraged the teachers to speak with her about her contributions to each of them, it is at least slightly likely, and more probably at least quite likely, that Mrs. Thompson would form the belief that she makes a real difference in the lives of her fellow teachers.

There is a second new belief that the principal might foster. Given her interest in technology, Mrs. Thompson is likely to evaluate favorably the opportunity to lead the school's integration of technology. The principal could offer her the chance to lead this project, with a choice of release time or extra pay funded by the technology grant. This offer might lead Mrs. Thompson to believe that she could lay the foundation for a career in educational technology at River Elementary. If she believed this strongly enough (+3), and if she evaluated it favorably enough (+3), this would make the strongest possible favorable contribution (+9) to her attitude toward the school.

Do you remember the rule that we can keep only about five to nine beliefs uppermost in our mind (or salient), at any one time? Therefore a maximum of only about five to nine beliefs can form our attitudes at any one time. Adding new beliefs to Mrs. Thompson's set of beliefs about her school will necessarily cause more weakly held beliefs to lose their salience, hence their influence on her attitude. As shown in Table 2.2, two weakly held beliefs ("Students uncooperative, hard to control," and "Chance to make real difference in students") have lost salience.

As a result of all these changes, Mrs. Thompson's attitude toward her school has improved markedly, from a very unfavorable −30, to a favorable +9.

CHAPTER SUMMARY

In this chapter, we have defined attitude, presented the two types of attitude, and discussed the two levels of attitude. We have seen how the MORA explains the formation of attitude toward an object, and we have investigated a case of attitude formation and change.

This case was of an attitude toward an object, an experienced teacher's attitude toward her school. Do you think an understanding of teachers' attitudes toward their school would be useful in planning specific steps to improve school culture or teacher morale? Would an understanding of teachers' attitudes toward a proposed policy in their school be useful in deciding whether or not to adopt the policy? Are there ways in which an understanding of students' attitudes toward their school would be helpful? Would it be useful for a district to understand likely voters' attitudes toward a school bond issue?

What attitudes toward objects are you interested in learning more about at your school or in your district?

How Are
Attitudes Toward
Behaviors Formed
and Changed?

BASIC CONCEPTS

Attitude Defined

Chapter 2 dealt with attitudes toward things, such as the schools in which we work, or people, such as teachers in our school. This chapter deals with attitudes, toward behaviors, such as reading this book to learn a new skill, or applying that new skill to learn about attitudes in your own school.

Attitudes toward behaviors can vary in both strength and direction. They can range from *extremely favorable* to *extremely unfavorable* through a neutral midpoint (*neither favorable nor unfavorable*). Attitude toward a behavior is formed by beliefs about outcomes of performing the behavior. This is discussed in more detail below.

Examples of *attitude toward a behavior* include parents' feelings about voting in favor of a school bond issue, principals' attitudes toward registering for professional development, teachers' feelings about enrolling in a graduate program, or students' feelings about volunteering to tutor their peers.

Levels of Attitude

There are *two levels* of attitude. The *first level* is a *global attitude,* such as "I *generally* like participating in professional development." The *second level* is a *specific attitude,* such as "I don't like the idea of having to participate in *that* workshop next Tuesday."

A global attitude toward a behavior (e.g., participating in professional development) cannot be expected to predict any specific behavior, although it will indicate a general behavioral predisposition. Students who like reading books voluntarily will probably read more books over the course of a year than students who do not like reading books. These avid readers, however, are not necessarily more likely to read any *specific* book than the nonreaders.

Formation of Attitude Toward a Behavior

Beliefs About Outcomes

As we consider performing a behavior, whether as trivial as watching a certain old movie on TV or as serious as leaving the field of education, we automatically begin to think about likely outcomes of our performing that behavior. The *salient* outcome beliefs that are uppermost in our minds are the ones important for forming attitude toward a behavior.

We will consider some of these outcomes as more likely than others to result from the behavior. We will see some outcomes as *extremely likely,* others as only *slightly likely,* and still others as somewhere in between. Based on differences in the information they have, different people will have somewhat different sets of outcome beliefs, and not all people will agree on the likelihood of any given outcome.

The strength and direction of outcome beliefs (and beliefs about the qualities of objects) are measured by the scale shown below. Although people do not form beliefs that they think are unlikely, the scale measures likelihood in both directions, so that people who do *not* believe in the likelihood of an outcome can indicate their disbelief.

extremely likely ___:___:___:___:___:___:___ extremely unlikely

For example, if we're thinking about watching an old Arnold Schwarzenegger movie on TV, we will probably expect—based on experience or on having read movie reviews—to see lots of action, and in his later movies, a certain amount of humor. If we're thinking about leaving the field of education, we form certain expectations about outcomes of leaving, based on the information we have read about, or hearing of the experiences of other educators who have left the field.

As we consider performing a behavior that we know a lot about (e.g., teaching a lesson on the causes of World War II), we will automatically think of between five and nine outcomes of performing that behavior. As we consider performing a behavior about which we know very little (e.g., reviewing a new software program on fractals), we are likely to think of fewer outcomes.

Evaluations of Outcomes

We not only make assumptions about likely outcomes, but we also automatically make evaluations of each outcome, based on our own long-term values and our immediate concerns. Our evaluations can range from *extremely good* to *extremely bad*, through a neutral midpoint (*neither good nor bad*). The scale that follows can measure the strength and direction of evaluation of an outcome.

extremely good ___:___:___:___:___:___:___ extremely bad

Both probability and evaluative scales are scored as shown below. These scales are scored from +3 to represent the *extremely likely* or *extremely good* end of the continuum to −3 to represent the *extremely unlikely* or *extremely bad* end of the continuum, through a neutral midpoint of zero (*neither likely nor unlikely, neither good nor bad*).

extremely $\underline{+3}$: $\underline{+2}$: $\underline{+1}$: $\underline{0}$: $\underline{-1}$: $\underline{-2}$: $\underline{-3}$ extremely

Belief-Evaluation Products

The multiplication of the strength of our belief in the likelihood of an outcome, and our evaluation of that outcome, is the belief-evaluation product. This product determines the direction and strength of that outcome's contribution toward attitude.

For example, if we believe that it is only *slightly likely* (+1) that going to a staff development workshop will help us learn something useful, even though we believe that learning something useful is *extremely good* (+3), the belief-evaluation product will only be +3. This will make a small, positive contribution to our attitude.

If, however, we read a brochure on the workshop that includes testimonials from people we respect, we might believe it to be *quite likely* (+2) that we would learn something at the workshop. This would double the product (from +3 to +6) and therefore double the positive contribution of that outcome to our attitude toward attending the workshop.

The process of formation of attitude toward a behavior by beliefs about outcomes of the behavior (and evaluations of those outcomes) is illustrated in Figure 3.1.

Attitude Change

Attitudes toward behaviors can be most effectively influenced, in the desired direction, only by knowing how those attitudes were formed. Once you have this understanding, there are three ways in which this knowledge can be used to influence attitudes, intentions, and behavior in the desired

Figure 3.1   Formation of Attitude Toward a Behavior

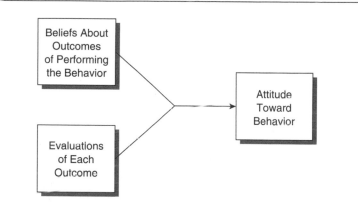

direction. The example given below illustrates how these three ways can be used.

CASE STUDY 2: FORMATION AND CHANGE OF ATTITUDE TOWARD RESIGNING

Formation of Favorable Attitude Toward Resigning From Teaching

As Mrs. Thompson thinks about resigning from teaching to pursue a master's in computer science, she automatically begins thinking about a number of likely outcomes, as reported in Table 3.1. She sees some of these outcomes as more likely to follow her resignation than others.

Some of these outcomes she evaluates favorably: getting more intellectual stimulation, getting away from this school, and having more time with her own children. Other outcomes she evaluates negatively: missing her students and fellow teachers, lower pay while working part-time as a graduate student, and having to spend time studying after being away from college for eight years. She evaluates some more strongly than others. For example, she evaluates "missing fellow teachers" more unfavorably than "missing my students," which she evaluates more unfavorably than "lower pay."

Table 3.1   Formation of Mrs. Thompson's Attitude Toward Resigning (*Before Intervention*)

Outcome	Belief	Evaluation	Product
More intellectual stimulation	+3	+3	+9
Will get me away from this school	+3	+2	+6
More time with my own children	+2	+2	+4
Will miss my students	+2	−2	−4
Will miss fellow teachers	+2	−3	−6
Lower pay	+3	−1	−3
Will have to spend time studying	+3	−1	−3
		Attitude = +3	

Note: Belief and evaluation scales are scored from +3 (*extremely likely, extremely favorable*) to −3 (*extremely unlikely, extremely unfavorable*) through a neutral midpoint (*neither*) of zero.

The strength of her beliefs about outcomes of resigning and the strength and direction of her evaluations of those outcomes combine to form her somewhat favorable attitude toward resigning. However, we don't always want *favorable* attitudes! We definitely don't want favorable attitudes toward *negative* (undesirable) behaviors!

If *you* were Mrs. Thompson's principal, and you saw Table 3.1, what would you do to influence her attitude in the desired direction, toward a *negative* attitude toward resigning?

Change to Unfavorable Attitude Toward Resigning From Teaching

First Way to Change

Contrary to the first case study, here we have a favorable attitude toward resigning, which the principal would like to change to an unfavorable attitude. The first way to change attitude in an *unfavorable direction* is to *reduce the strength of one or more of the positively evaluated outcomes*. Are all of these outcomes really likely?

The third outcome is probably untrue, as it is unlikely that a full-time graduate student with a part-time job and some domestic responsibilities would have *more* free time for her children than a full-time teacher who is not studying for a degree. By reminding Mrs. Thompson of this, the principal might reduce the strength of this belief from +2 to +1, as shown in Table 3.2, reducing the contribution of that outcome-evaluation product to attitude. Belief in the first two outcomes, however, seems realistic.

If the principal had been successful in changing Mrs. Thompson's attitude toward the school in a favorable direction, as illustrated in Chapter 2, the evaluation of the second outcome, "Get me away from this school," will become less favorable, and perhaps even negative. This would reduce the positive contribution of the outcome to attitude, or even reverse it, so that it makes a negative contribution to her attitude toward resigning.

The first outcome, "More intellectual stimulation," offers the principal numerous opportunities. The principal could offer Mrs. Thompson release time two half days per week to lead an effort to more fully integrate technology into the school's instruction. The principal could inform Mrs. Thompson about the district's newly developed partnership with the state university, which offers a master's degree in educational technology. Most classes will be taught in the district's professional development center, and teachers can take one course per semester while keeping their jobs. Either or both of these items of information could significantly reduce, or eliminate, Mrs. Thompson's belief that resigning would bring her more intellectual stimulation would than staying in teaching.

Second Way to Change

The second to way to change attitude in an *unfavorable direction* is to *strengthen beliefs in negatively evaluated outcomes.* There are four of these, but missing her students and her fellow teachers make stronger positive contributions, so let's focus on them.

Table 3.2   Change of Mrs. Thompson's Attitude Toward
Resigning (*After Intervention*)

Outcome	Belief	Evaluation	Product
Old Beliefs			
More intellectual stimulation	~~+3~~ 0	+3	~~+9~~ 0
Will get me away from this school	+3	+2 −2	~~+6~~ −6
More time with my own children	~~+2~~ +1	+2	~~+4~~ +2
Will miss my students	+2	−2	−4
Will miss fellow teachers	~~+2~~ +3	−3	~~−6~~ −9
Lower pay	+3	−1	−3
Will have to spend time studying	+3	−1	−3

Old Attitude = ~~+3~~ −23

	Belief	Evaluation	Product
New Beliefs			
Lose opportunity for district master's	+3	−2	−6
Lose opportunity to lead tech project	+3	−3	−9

New Beliefs = −15

New Attitude = −38

Note: Belief and evaluation scales are scored from +3 (*extremely likely, extremely favorable*) to −3 (*extremely unlikely,* or *extremely, unfavorable*) through a neutral midpoint (*neither*) of zero.

Suppose that Mrs. Thompson likes the idea of leading a tech-integration project among her fellow teachers (and that they had come to her, as in the case study in Chapter 2, and told her how important to them she was). This might increase the likelihood (from +2 to +3) that she would miss her fellow teachers if she resigned. That change would increase the negative contribution of the outcome "will miss fellow teachers" from −6 to −9.

These changes in beliefs (and in one outcome evaluation) have dramatically changed Mrs. Thompson's attitude toward resigning, from a slightly favorable +3 to a much stronger unfavorable −23.

But there is more work yet to be done.

Third Way to Change

The third way to change attitude in an *unfavorable direction* is to *add new beliefs* about outcomes that Mrs. Thompson will negatively evaluate to her salient set of outcome beliefs. The principal has already done this by offering Mrs. Thompson leadership of the tech-integration project and the opportunity to study for a master's in educational technology. Many other possibilities exist for adding incentives that will be favorably evaluated.

As seen in Table 3.2, with the changes in the old beliefs and the addition of two new beliefs about outcomes that are unfavorably evaluated, Mrs. Thompson's attitude toward resigning is noticeably more negative (the desired direction) than before the principal's intervention. Mrs. Thompson is, therefore, *less* likely to resign (assuming that her intention is influenced by attitude).

CHAPTER SUMMARY

In this chapter, we have defined attitude toward a behavior and discussed the two levels of this attitude. We have seen how the MORA shows how attitude toward a behavior is formed, and we have investigated a case of attitude formation and change. This case was of an experienced teacher's attitude toward resigning from her school.

- Do you think an understanding of teachers' attitudes toward resigning from their schools would be useful in planning specific steps to improve teacher retention?
- What other teacher behaviors would be important for school improvement? What student behaviors would be important? What parent or community behaviors?
- What attitudes toward behaviors are you interested in learning more about at your school?

4

How Is Perceived Social Pressure Formed and Changed?

BASIC CONCEPTS

Norm Defined

As discussed in Chapter 1, decisions about behavior are formed by a *personal* factor, attitude, as well as a *social* factor, subjective norm. Norm is our perception that those people or groups who are important to us would favor—or oppose—our performing the behavior. In other words, it is our perception of the behavioral expectations of those who are important to us.

We call this norm *subjective,* because people will often never hear *directly* what their "important others" want them to do or not do in a given situation. Instead, they will usually *infer* the expectations of these persons and groups, based on what they know about each of their "important others" and what they know about the behavior under consideration.

Relative Importance of Attitude and Norm

Although both factors *can* be important in forming intention, attitude is usually more important. Sometimes, however, subjective norm is the only factor that determines behavioral intention. What accounts for the relative influence of attitudinal and normative influences on intentions?

There is evidence from research to suggest that in behavioral domains in which the people being studied have a lot of information about the behavior (e.g., mandatory testing), attitude is the more important factor. Sometimes, it is the only significant influence on intention. In domains in which people have *less* information (e.g., technology integration), subjective norm becomes relatively more important.

Some studies have shown differences in the relative influence of attitude and norm, based on the sex of those studied. Personality type might also be important in determining the relative weights. It seems intuitive that extroverted people might be relatively more influenced by normative considerations than would introverted people.

The relative influence depends on a number of factors: (a) the people being studied, (b) the behavior of interest, (c) the importance of the behavior to those being studied, and (d) possibly other factors. The implication is that whenever you are interested in how people are forming their decisions about some behavior, the only way to be sure about the relative weights of attitude and norm is to study the people and behavior of concern.

Formation of Norm

Normative Beliefs

Norm is formed by a set of beliefs about the likely expectations of people and groups who are important to us. For the sake of brevity, these persons or groups are referred to below as *referents* (we *refer* to their expectations when considering our behavior).

We will have different referents for different behaviors, behavioral categories, behavioral contexts, and so forth. For example, our referents for the behavioral category of "cutting the grass regularly" will likely include immediate family and neighbors. Distant relatives across the country, coworkers, and supervisors will probably not matter to us.

However, consider the behavior of "registering for a professional development workshop." In this case, we are most likely to be concerned with the expectations of those with whom we work. We probably won't think about what our neighbors or distant relatives might want us to do. We might well consider, however, what our immediate family might want us to do. Normative beliefs are measured by a probability scale such as the one that follows.

My family wants me to enroll in the district master's degree course

extremely likely __:__:__:__:__ : __ extremely unlikely

Motivation to Comply

Are we likely to be equally motivated by the desires of all referents? Most likely we are not. As would be expected, we have found that, at least for school-related behaviors, teachers are typically most motivated to comply with the expectations of their principals, somewhat motivated to comply with other teachers, and less motivated to comply with the expectations of their students. In behaviors around the home, they will likely be most motivated to comply with members of their immediate family, somewhat less with neighbors, and even less with distant relatives. Motivation to comply is traditionally measured by a probability scale such as the following.

Usually, I want to do what my family wants me to do

extremely likely __:__:__:__:__:__ extremely unlikely

However, given the research on opinion seeking that shows people seek the opinions of those they perceive as knowing more about a subject, it might make sense to measure motivation to comply within a behavioral domain, for example, the first scale that follows, or even the specific behavior, as in the second scale.

When it comes to my career, I want to do what my family wants me to do

extremely likely ___:___:___:___:___:___ extremely unlikely

When it comes to my enrolling in a master's program, I want to do what my family wants me to do

extremely likely ___:___:___:___:___:___ extremely unlikely

The formation of subjective norm by normative beliefs and motivations to comply is illustrated in Figure 4.1.

To summarize, subjective norm is the combination of our beliefs about the desires of each of our referents and our motivation to comply with each of those referents. The more strongly we believe a given referent would favor (or oppose) our performing a behavior, and the more motivated we are to comply with that referent, the stronger that referent's contribution to our perception of social pressure regarding the behavior.

Change of Norm

The norm of a group can be changed in the desired direction in three ways. The *first* way focuses on negative referents, those who are perceived as *not* favoring the performance of a desired behavior. This approach targets the strength of normative beliefs and attempts to reduce the strength of beliefs about the expectations of those referents. (If, as in our example, the behavior is *not* desired, then this way attempts to *increase* the strength of normative beliefs.)

Figure 4.1   Formation of Social Pressure Regarding a Behavior

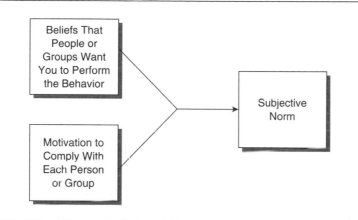

The *second* way focuses on positive referents, those perceived as favoring the performance of the desired behavior. This approach involves increasing the strength of normative beliefs that these referents favor the behavior. (In our example here, the behavior is *not* desired, and this way attempts to *decrease* the strength of normative beliefs.)

The *third* way is to add new referents to the salient set who would favor the group's performing the desired behavior. (In our example, the behavior is *not* desired, and this way attempts to add new referents who would *oppose* the behavior.) Now let's return to our example of Mrs. Thompson and her initial consideration of resignation from teaching at River Elementary School.

CASE STUDY 3: FORMATION AND CHANGE OF NORM TOWARD RESIGNING

Formation of Mrs. Thompson's Norm to Favor Resigning

Remember that *before* her principal intervened with information to influence the decision, Mrs. Thompson had formed a slightly favorable attitude toward resigning. As demonstrated in Table 3.1, this attitude was based on favorable evaluations of three outcomes and unfavorable evaluations of four outcomes of resigning. She believed all seven outcomes were at least *quite likely* (+2). She liked the outcomes of getting more intellectual stimulation, getting away from River Elementary, and having more time with her own children. She disliked, however, the outcomes of missing her students and fellow teachers at River Elementary, receiving lower pay while working part-time during her graduate studies, and having to spend time studying.

As demonstrated in Table 4.1, Mrs. Thompson initially thought it only *slightly likely* (+1) that her husband would favor her resignation. This was because she believed that although he would like the intellectual stimulation and greater opportunities and salary that a master's in computer science would bring her, she knew he would miss the contribution her salary makes at a tough time in the family's finances. Although her motivation to comply with her husband is not the highest possible (+6), at +5 it is still quite high.

Mrs. Thompson believed that her own children would like her to be home more, and she is motivated to comply with them. She believed that her fellow teachers, her students, and her principal do *not* favor her resignation, but she is less motivated to comply with their expectations than with her family's expectations.

Change of Mrs. Thompson's Norm to Oppose Resigning

Mrs. Thompson's principal created new opportunities for her at River Elementary and provided other information that helped to influence her attitude toward resigning from slightly favorable (+3) to quite unfavorable (−38). How might these attitudinal changes have influenced Mrs. Thompson's perception of normative pressure about resigning?

As shown in Table 3.2, the principal's intervention directly influenced Mrs. Thompson's beliefs about two referents

Table 4.1   Formation of Mrs. Thompson's Subjective Norm
(*Before Intervention*)

Referent	Belief	Motivation to Comply	Product
Spouse	+1	+5	+5
My children	+2	+4	+8
Fellow teachers	-2	+3	-6
My students	-2	+2	-4
My principal	-3	0	0
		Subjective Norm =	+3

Note: Beliefs about referents' expectations can range from +3 to -3. Motivation to comply with a given referent can range from +6 (*extremely motivated*) to 0 (*not at all motivated*).

("My children" and "Fellow teachers"). After the intervention, she believed it less likely that resigning would give her more time with her own children. Her fellow teachers telling her how important she was to them made it more likely that she would miss her fellow teachers.

The behavior of interest here (resigning from teaching) is *not* desired by the principal. This means that the three ways of influencing norm discussed earlier are just a bit different from when the behavior is desired. It seems just about as likely that school leaders will want to prevent behaviors (e.g., teachers resigning, students dropping out) as promoting them (e.g., teachers integrating technology, students taking more advanced placement courses).

In this example, the *first* way focuses on negative referents (i.e., those who are perceived as *not* favoring the performance of a desired behavior) and attempts to *increase* the strength of normative beliefs. As shown in Table 4.2, having her fellow teachers tell her how important she is to them increased the strength of Mrs. Thompson's belief that those teachers did not want her to resign. This change altered the belief-motivation product for "fellow teachers" from -6 to -9. The extra efforts

Table 4.2   Change of Mrs. Thompson's Subjective Norm
(*After Intervention*)

Referent	Belief	Motivation to Comply	Product
Old Beliefs			
Spouse	+1	+5	+5
My children	~~+2~~ +1	+4	~~+8~~ +4
Fellow teachers	~~-2~~ +3	+3	~~-6~~ -9
My students	-2	+2	-4
My principal	-3	~~-0~~ +1	~~-0~~ -3
		Old Subjective Norm =	~~+3~~ -7
New Beliefs			
Tech. Assoc. teachers	-2	+2	-4
District tech. coord.	-2	+1	-2
		New Beliefs =	-6
		New Subjective Norm =	-13

Note: Beliefs about referents' expectations can range from +3 to −3. Motivation to comply with a given referent can range from +6 (*extremely motivated*) to 0 (*not at all motivated*).

undertaken to retain her lead Mrs. Thompson toward a more favorable opinion of the principal and toward a slightly greater willingness to comply with expectations.

The *second* way focuses on positive referents, those perceived as favoring the performance of the behavior, and attempts to *decrease* the strength of normative beliefs. After Mrs. Thompson realized that resigning was not very likely to increase her time with her own children, she also came to believe less strongly that her children would want her to resign.

Thus far these changes alone have moved Mrs. Thompson's perception of normative pressure from slightly favorable (+3) to somewhat unfavorable (−7). However, still more can be done.

The *third* way is to add new referents to the salient set. In our example, this way attempts to add referents who would *oppose* the behavior. As Mrs. Thompson begins thinking about leading the technology integration project at her school, she begins to think about other people who might have an opinion of her leading that effort. She infers that her "techie" friends at other schools across the state, whom she knows through the state educational technology association, would favor her leading the project, and she is fairly motivated to comply with those teachers. She also infers that her district's technology coordinator would favor her leading the project and that attention from the district office could be a stepping-stone to other opportunities.

CHAPTER SUMMARY

In this chapter, we have defined subjective norm concerning a behavior. We have seen how the MORA shows how subjective norm is formed, and we have investigated a case of normative formation and change. This case was of an experienced teacher's norm concerning her resignation from her school.

- Do you think an understanding of teachers' perceptions of normative pressure about resigning from their schools would be useful in planning specific steps to improve teacher retention?
- What other teacher norms concerning behaviors would be important for school improvement?
- What student behaviors would be important?
- What parent or community behaviors?
- What kinds of normative pressure are you interested in learning more about at your school?

Putting It
All Together

The Model as a Whole

HOW WE MAKE DECISIONS ABOUT OUR BEHAVIOR: ATTITUDE AND NORM

We saw in Chapter 1 that the model of reasoned action (MORA) shows that people make decisions about their behavior based on a personal factor and a social factor.

- The personal factor is our attitude toward performing the behavior; our positive, negative, or neutral feeling about the behavior.
- The social factor is our subjective norm, our perception of social pressure concerning the behavior.

The relative influence of attitude and norm will vary depending upon the population of decision makers, the behavior and context, and other factors. Figure 5.1 shows the factors and relationships among those factors that compose the model.

Figure 5.1   The Model of Reasoned Action

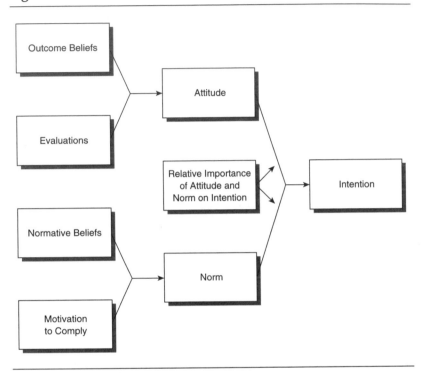

Attitude

We saw in Chapter 3 how Mrs. Thompson's attitude toward resigning from River Elementary School was formed by a set of beliefs about the likely outcomes of resigning to pursue a master's degree and her evaluations of each outcome. As shown in Table 3.1, she favorably evaluated three outcomes of resigning: (a) "More intellectual stimulation," (b) "Will get me away from this school," and (c) "More time with my own children."

She unfavorably evaluated four outcomes: (a) "Will miss my students," (b) "Will miss fellow teachers," (c) "Lower pay" (as a graduate student and part-time worker), and (d) "Will have to spend time studying" (after so many years away from college), Taken together, these beliefs and evaluations resulted in a slightly favorable attitude toward resigning, a behavior that her principal did not want.

Based on an understanding of these outcome beliefs and evaluations, Mrs. Thompson's principal intervened with action and information designed to influence her attitude in a negative direction (away from resigning). As shown in Table 3.2, the principal used all three methods for influencing attitude. First, the principal succeeded in lowering the strength of beliefs about favorably evaluated outcomes ("More intellectual stimulation," "More time with my own children") and changed the evaluation of one outcome ("Will get me away from this school") from positive to negative.

Second, the principal increased the strength of belief in a negatively evaluated outcome ("Will miss fellow teachers"). These changes reduced a slightly favorable attitude (+3) toward resigning to a strongly negative attitude (−23).

Third, by providing two new opportunities for her, the principal introduced two new beliefs about outcomes that Mrs. Thompson was likely to evaluate negatively ("Lose opportunity for district master's," "Lose opportunity to lead tech project"). These two new beliefs further influence attitude in a negative direction by another −15 points, from −23 to −38.

Subjective Norm

We saw in Chapter 4 how Mrs. Thompson's subjective norm was formed by a set of beliefs that people or groups who are important to her (referents) favored—or opposed—her resigning and her motivation to comply with each referent. (The norm is subjective because she did not hear *directly* from her referents what they expected her to do, but rather she inferred their expectations based on what she knows of them and what she knows about resigning from teaching.)

As shown in Table 4.1, Mrs. Thompson initially thought her spouse and children would favor her resigning, and she was motivated to comply with them. She believed that her fellow teachers, her students, and her principal would oppose her resigning, but Mrs. Thompson was less motivated to comply with them.

Based on an understanding of these normative beliefs and motivations to comply, Mrs. Thompson's principal intervened with action and information designed to influence her norm in a negative direction (away from resigning). As shown in Table 4.2, the principal used all three methods for influencing norm. First, the principal succeeded in lowering the strength of belief that her own children wanted her to resign.

Second, the principal increased the strength of belief that her fellow teachers would oppose her resigning. The principal's efforts to make her happy and to feel important, as well as the new opportunity to lead a tech-integration effort, made Mrs. Thompson feel more favorably toward the principal and slightly more motivated to comply with the principal. These changes alone reduced a slightly favorable norm (+3) to a slightly negative norm (−7).

Third, by providing two new opportunities for her, the principal introduced two new beliefs about referents who would be likely to *oppose* Mrs. Thompson's resigning, and with whom she was likely to be motivated to comply (teachers in the state educational technology association and the district technology coordinator). These two additions to the referent belief set further reduced norm by −6, resulting in a much more negative norm of −13.

CHAPTER SUMMARY

In this chapter, we have reviewed how the strength of our beliefs about the likely outcomes of a behavior and our evaluation of each outcome combine to form our attitude toward the behavior.

We have further reviewed how the strength of our beliefs about the likely preferences for our behavior of each of a set of referents combined with the degree of our motivation to comply with each referent form our subjective norm.

Together, attitude and norm form our intention to perform—or to not perform—the behavior. The relative influence of attitude and norm will differ according to the population of decision makers, the behavior of interest, and other variables.

- *Whose* behavioral intentions are important to your school's success?
- *What* behaviors would you *most* like to influence?

PART II

Conducting
Your Study

Narrowing
Your Interest

FROM A PROBLEM OR OPPORTUNITY
TO A RESEARCHABLE QUESTION

In our schools today, we are faced with both problems and opportunities. Examples of problems include high teacher attrition, high student dropout rates, and low parental involvement in students' education. Examples of opportunities might include a new bond issue to fund technology integration, interest among some parents in increasing their involvement with the school, and a chance to gain financial support for athletics from local businesses. Let's refer to both problems and opportunities as "concerns."

Before you can use the model of reasoned action (MORA), however, you must refine your concern into a researchable question. This chapter will take you through these necessary steps, beginning with the people you want to understand and influence, and concluding with the four behavioral elements: behavior, context, time, and target.

Population of Interest

The first question is *whose* behavior are you interested in? Is it teachers, students, parents of your students, or voters in your district?

- If teachers, *which* teachers? All teachers in a certain grade level across the district, all teachers in a school building, or all teachers who have fewer than five years' service in the district?
- If parents, *which* parents? Parents of middle school students (the period when parental involvement begins to drop off), parents of middle school students whose grades were below a C average for the last three quarters, or parents of middle school students who have below-average GPAs and play sports?
- If voters in your district, *which* voters? Is it all registered voters? Or all registered voters who voted in the last election? Or just registered voters who voted in the last bond issue election? Be sure to refine this group to *exactly* the people whose behavior you are interested in, and no one else.

At this point, it might be good to think of the background characteristics of these people that might make a difference in their thinking or behavior. By including these characteristics in your study questionnaire, you will be able to examine differences in beliefs, attitudes, norms, and intentions among different categories of people.

For example, on a given policy, will women have a different viewpoint from men? Will older people have different intentions than younger people? Will highly experienced teachers view things differently from newer teachers?

Sex, age, employment status, years of experience, current highest degree, and marital or parental status are background characteristics often employed in studies. Your review of the relevant literature, brainstorming with others concerned with the situation, or discussion with your district research director can help you identify the background characteristics you need to include.

Behavior

If you want to study behavioral intentions, what exactly do you want to know about? When thinking about the focus of your study, it is important to distinguish among single behaviors, behavioral categories, and behavioral outcomes. The definitions and examples below might be helpful in keeping these distinctions straight.

Single Behaviors

A single behavior is an act that you can watch someone perform. Examples include drinking a cup of black coffee, walking up a flight of stairs, and parking a car at the far end of the parking lot.

Behavioral Categories

A behavioral category is a group of behaviors performed with a given outcome in mind, such as "dieting" or "getting fit." You can't watch a person dieting or getting fit.

If, however, you knew that our friend Dr. Bernard usually drinks his coffee with cream, and you saw him drinking a cup of black coffee; and if you knew that he usually takes the elevator, and you saw him walking up a flight of stairs; and if you knew that he usually parks as close to the building as possible, and you saw him parking at the far end of the parking lot, you might infer that he was trying to get fit.

When we see a number of behaviors performed by the same person, depending on what we know about the person performing the behaviors, we infer that the behaviors are intended with a single outcome in mind and that they make up a behavioral category.

Behavioral Outcomes

A behavioral outcome is the purpose for which a behavior is performed. When our friend Dr. Bernard drinks black coffee instead of coffee with cream, walks up the stairs instead of taking the elevator, and parks at the far end of the parking lot instead of next to the building, he is hoping to "get fit," and whether he achieves that or not, that is the end he has in mind.

There are three other elements that are important to our thinking about a behavior, behavioral category, or behavioral outcome:

- The context
- The time
- The target of the behavior

Context of Behavior

The context in which a behavior (or category of behaviors) is to be performed can greatly affect our thinking about it. For example, think about the behavior of working on a report while wearing shorts and a T-shirt. In the context of working at home, this will probably make sense to you and be comfortable.

Put this behavior in the context of working at the office, however, and it will probably be highly *un*comfortable! One thing is certain: The kind of normative pressure you will feel when considering this behavior will certainly be different in the two contexts!

Time of Behavior

The time at which a behavior (or category of behaviors) is to be performed can also greatly affect our thinking about it. For example, you might very well have a favorable attitude toward going to see a movie at 7:00 P.M., but an *un*favorable attitude toward seeing the same movie at the midnight showing.

You might have a favorable attitude toward going to school a little early to finish up some work at, say, 6:30 A.M., but have a very *un*favorable attitude toward going in at 3:30 A.M.

Target of Behavior

The target of a behavior can also affect our thinking about performing a behavior. For example, a student might have a favorable attitude toward going to school a little early to help his favorite teacher set up her biology experiment, but have a very *un*favorable attitude toward going in at the same time of day to help a less favored teacher set up his chemistry experiment.

CHAPTER SUMMARY

In this chapter, we have seen five ways to refine a problem or opportunity into a highly researchable question.

- First, you need to be very specific about the people in whom you are interested.
- Second, you need to be very specific about the behavior (or behavioral category, or behavioral outcome) in which you are interested.
- Third, you need to be very specific about the context of the behavior in which you are interested.
- Fourth, you need to be very specific about the time during which the behavior in which you are interested will be performed.
- Fifth, you need to be very specific about the target of the behavior in which you are interested.

Collecting
Your Data

SIX STEPS TO DATA COLLECTION

This chapter will take you through the six steps for collecting data for your study using the entire model of reasoned action (MORA):

- Selecting your samples
- Eliciting outcome and normative beliefs
- Selecting beliefs common to the population
- Developing the scales for your questionnaire
- Adding questions external to the model
- Testing your questionnaire

These steps can also be applied—with modification of the belief-elicitation questions—to studying an attitude toward an object, such as a proposed school or district policy.

Step 1: Selecting Your Samples

Once you have refined your research question, as discussed in the previous chapter, you will know *exactly* the specific group of people from which you want to collect data. From this point, it is fairly simple to determine how best to reach a reasonably sized sample that will be representative of the population.

First, you will need to select a representative sample, preferably a random sample, of those who will receive the final written questionnaire. Second, from this first group, you should randomly draw a subsample of perhaps 50–100 people. This subsample will be the group from whom you elicit the beliefs that underlie attitude and norm. These beliefs will be used to develop the scales on the final questionnaire.

Step 2: Eliciting the Beliefs
That Underlie Attitude and Norm

Beliefs can be elicited in several ways: by interview (whether in person or by telephone), by focused group interview, or by written questionnaire with open-ended response items. There are advantages and disadvantages to each method.

As the purpose is to elicit *only* those beliefs that are salient (uppermost in the minds of the people being studied), group interviews can present a problem. Beliefs mentioned by one person might lead other people to infer beliefs that previously were not salient. When the questionnaire is administered to the general sample, therefore, the correlations between estimated and direct measures of attitude (or norm) will be low, indicating that the belief set that is modally salient was not fully captured during the elicitation process. Although group interviews are a potential problem, they *can* provide adequate results.

Written questionnaires are probably the easiest way to elicit belief data, and they are less likely to result in social desirability bias in responses than interviews are. There can be problems, however, with using a questionnaire. The worst problem is that respondents sometimes write extremely brief statements, which are quite difficult to understand. Especially for outcome beliefs, these can be very difficult to interpret. (Fortunately, normative beliefs are nearly always straight-forward.) However, if telephone follow-up interviews can be conducted to clarify remarks that are unclear, this can be a good method of eliciting beliefs.

In-person interviews have many advantages, most espe-cially that of allowing you to query respondents when their responses are unclear. However, they also have the greatest likelihood of producing social desirability bias, and they take a considerable amount of time to conduct. Telephone inter-views should be a bit easier to conduct, and they produce less social desirability bias than interviews in person. They still provide the opportunity to clarify statements elicited from respondents.

Regardless of the data collection method chosen, three questions are asked to elicit the beliefs underlying attitude toward a behavior:

- What are the advantages of your doing . . . [the behavior]?
- What are the *dis*advantages of your doing . . . [the behavior]?
- What else comes to mind when you think about doing . . . [the behavior]?

Three questions are asked to elicit the beliefs underlying subjective norm concerning a behavior:

- What persons or groups might be *in favor of* your doing . . . [the behavior]?
- What persons or groups might be *opposed to* your doing . . . [the behavior]?
- Who else might have an opinion about your doing . . . [the behavior]?

If you elicit beliefs by written questionnaire, ask respon-dents to number each separate belief. This will help at the next step of data collection. If you elicit beliefs by interview, you might take notes on a legal pad or laptop computer. You will probably get about three to six outcome beliefs from each person, for a total of perhaps several hundred separate belief statements.

Step 3: Selecting a Set of Salient Beliefs Common to the Population

Once outcome and normative beliefs have been elicited, the next task is organizing these data. (The discussion below applies primarily to the selection of outcome beliefs, because these are more numerous and less straightforward than normative beliefs.)

Even in a fairly homogenous group (e.g., special education teachers with over five years' experience), different people will have somewhat different beliefs about likely outcomes of a behavior. To allow comparison across the entire group, you must create a set of salient beliefs that is common to the group as a whole.

Organizing Beliefs

The next step in creating a set of salient beliefs that is common to the group as a whole is organizing the beliefs. This means grouping together beliefs that refer to similar outcomes and counting the frequency with which they occur.

Given that you could have hundreds of beliefs, you might want to put each separate belief (outcome and normative) on an individual piece of paper before trying to organize them. Entering all the beliefs into a computer might be effective, but I (BWP) have found 3 × 5 cards best for grouping these beliefs. Because you can have anywhere from 15 to 30 piles of cards at the beginning, I like to have plenty of space to spread out, such as a large kitchen table.

Once you have written each separate belief statement on a separate card, you can begin laying out the cards on a large table, *grouping similar statements into piles.* Once you have read all the cards and put most of them into one of the piles, you can go over the organization and review once again those cards that you initially couldn't decide on. (Some beliefs will likely be mentioned by so few people, and be so different from any other beliefs, that they must remain in a "miscellaneous" pile.)

Let us begin with the *partial* list of hypothetical outcome beliefs that could have been produced by a subsample of 75 teachers in Table 7.1. These 19 beliefs are organized into five groups on the basis of their similarity.

Deciding What Is the Same and What Is Different

The next task is deciding which belief statements really concern the same outcome and which refer to truly different, though similar, outcomes. Some differences will really be just different ways of saying the same thing. For example, the beliefs in Group 1 all concern the same outcome but state this in different terms, and so we will merge them into one belief and use the most frequently mentioned wording for the combined belief.

In other cases, it will be less easy to decide whether the statements refer to similar or identical outcomes. In such cases, ask yourself if both beliefs could have come from the same person. Then check the responses to see how many respondents actually did mention both beliefs. If many respondents have mentioned both outcomes, they probably should be considered separate. If only a few respondents have mentioned both outcomes, those outcomes should probably be considered the same. For example, the beliefs in Group 4 are quite similar, but when we check the original responses, we find that many people have included at least two of the three beliefs, and we conclude that the respondents saw these three as truly unique outcomes.

Table 7.1   Organization of Salient Beliefs About Outcomes of
Resigning From Teaching

Belief Grouping	Outcome	Frequency	Belief Number
1	I will have more income	15	1
	I will get a better paying job	20	2
2	I will get a defined lunch hour	10	3
	I won't have summers off	15	4
	I will have to work weekends or nights	10	5
	I won't have to grade papers at night	30	6
	I won't have to grade papers on weekends	25	7
3	I will miss seeing how my students grow up	12	
	I will miss seeing how my students develop	8	8
	I will miss seeing students grow	5	
	I will miss seeing students learn as they mature	10	
4	I will meet more interesting people	13	9
	I will expand my social life	12	10
	I will get more interaction with adults	12	11
	More intellectual stimulation	20	12
5	I won't have yard duty	4	
	I won't have bus duty	5	13
	I won't have hall duty	3	
	I won't have lunchroom duty	4	

Grouping Related Beliefs Into a New Belief

Sometimes you will find a number of low-frequency beliefs that refer to quite similar but distinct outcomes. For example, the four outcomes in Group 5 concern four different, noninstructional responsibilities that annoy many teachers. Although only a few respondents have mentioned each of these, all four of them together refer to an outcome of resigning that might be salient for the group as a whole. This outcome of resigning could be labeled "I won't have any extraneous duties."

Deciding How Many Beliefs to Include

How many of the beliefs your respondents have elicited do you want to include in your instrument? The developers of the model (Ajzen & Fishbein, 1980, p. 70) offer three guidelines for deciding how many beliefs to include in the final set of salient beliefs that will represent the outcome beliefs of the group you are studying.

- A given frequency (e.g., the 10 or 12) of the most frequently mentioned beliefs
- The beliefs mentioned by a given percentage (e.g., at least 10% or 20%) of the belief-elicitation subsample
- A given percentage (e.g., 75%) of all beliefs elicited

Ajzen and Fishbein (1980) state that the third rule is perhaps the least arbitrary, and I (BWP) typically use that one.

Let us look at how each of these rules works with the full list of hypothetical beliefs about outcomes of resigning that could have been elicited by the subsample of 75 teachers in Table 7.2.

Using the first rule, including the ten most frequently elicited beliefs (belief numbers 1–10) gives us 238 beliefs, or a little fewer than 63% of all beliefs elicited. Including the 12 most frequently elicited beliefs (belief numbers 1–12) gives us 262 beliefs, or just over 69% of all beliefs elicited.

Using the second rule, including all beliefs elicited by 10% of respondents in the belief-elicitation subsample gives us all beliefs elicited by eight respondents or more (belief numbers 1–18). Limiting this rule to beliefs elicited by 20% of respondents gives us all beliefs elicited by 15 respondents or more (belief numbers 1–8).

Table 7.2   Identification of Common Salient Outcome Beliefs

Belief Number	Outcome	Frequency
1	I will miss seeing how my students grow up	35
2	I will get a better paying job	35
3	I will miss being in control of my own work	32
4	I won't have to grade papers at night	30
5	I won't have to grade papers on weekends	30
6	More intellectual stimulation	20
7	I won't have extraneous duties	16
8	I won't have summers off	15
9	I will meet more interesting people	13
10	I will expand my social life	12
11	I will get more interaction with adults	12
12	I will get a more attractive workplace	12
13	I will get more technical support	10
14	I will have to travel	10
15	I will get a defined lunch hour	10
16	I will be able to go back to school	10
17	I might have to work weekends or nights	10
18	I will get better working conditions	8
19	It will help me fulfill my potential	5
20	I will have a longer workday	5
Miscellaneous beliefs with frequencies below 5		48
	Total =	378

Using the third rule, including 75% of all beliefs elicited (283.5 beliefs), we could select the first 14 beliefs (which gives 282 beliefs, slightly fewer than 75%), or we could select the first 15 beliefs (which gives us 292 beliefs, considerably more than 75%). Note that use of the third rule provides a larger number of beliefs for the in-common set than any of the other rules except the second rule of 10%.

Normative Beliefs

Normative beliefs are typically more straightforward. Your respondents will mention referents, usually by their relationship to the respondent, as in "my husband," "my wife," "fellow teachers," "my principal," and so forth.

Some problems, however, might be found even with normative beliefs. In the belief-elicitation phases of a study of oral surgeons, some respondents mentioned that their peers would favor (or oppose) the behavior under investigation. Others mentioned that their colleagues would have an opinion. Are "peers" and "colleagues" the same?

When subsequent respondents were asked about the similarity, roughly half responded in the affirmative, about half in the negative. This issue was resolved by combining the two words and using "peers/colleagues" on the final questionnaire.

Step 4: Measuring the Beliefs
That Underlie Attitude and Norm

Once you have selected the salient outcome beliefs that are held in common by the group you are interested in, you have finished the most difficult part of using this model. It's smooth sailing from here on! Now, just follow the tips below to create your instrument.

Attitude

- Type each outcome belief statement, using the exact wording of most respondents who mentioned it. Now randomize the order of these outcome statements, copy the entire list, and put that second list of beliefs aside.

- Type an evaluative scale such as the one below:

extremely good ___:___:___:___:___:___:___ extremely bad

- Copy the evaluative scale beneath each outcome belief statement in the first list. These scales will allow your respondents to evaluate each outcome.
- Type a probability scale such as the one below:

extremely likely ___:___:___:___:___:___:___ extremely unlikely

- Next, copy the probability scale beneath each outcome belief statement in the second list. These scales will allow your respondents to rate the likelihood that each outcome will result from their performance of the behavior.

Subjective Norm

- Type each normative belief statement, using the exact wording of most respondents who mentioned it.
- Randomize the order of these normative belief statements.
- Copy the names of the referents in exactly the same order as the normative belief statements.
- Copy a probability scale, such as the one below, beneath each referent (as shown in this example) to measure motivation to comply.

Usually, I want to do what my family wants me to do

extremely likely ___:___:___:___:___:___:___ extremely unlikely

- Copy another probability scale, such as the one below, beneath each referent (as shown in this example) to measure normative belief.

My family wants me to enroll in the district master's degree course

extremely likely __:__:__:__:__:__:__ extremely unlikely

Remember that it is critical to maintain the same level of specificity, concerning the behavior, throughout the entire data collection process, from belief elicitation, to final instrument. Remember the four behavioral elements of behavior, context, time, and target, discussed in the previous chapter. If you begin by asking about "resigning from teaching in the next two years," then you must maintain this *exact* time frame throughout the questionnaire.

Step 5: Adding Variables External to the Model

Chapter 6 described some of the most important ways in which you need to refine your research question, beginning with the "Population of Interest." Once you have refined your study question, you will have a general sense of what background information you want to collect on your respondents with your final questionnaire. There are three reasons for collecting background information from your respondents.

First, you will want to be able to screen out any respondents who you don't really want. For example, suppose you are interested in teachers who are five years away from retirement. If a novice teacher somehow gets into the respondent pool, you will want to be able to exclude that person's responses before analyzing the data.

Second, you will probably want to compare respondents on background variables. For example, you might want to compare the responses of teachers who were trained in a traditional teacher preparation program versus teachers who were trained in a postbaccalaureate program. Other background variables on teachers might be grade level taught, years of experience, current highest degree, and so forth.

Third, you will probably want to compare respondents on other variables external to the model. Among these other variables might be future behaviors that they might, or might not, perform (e.g., enrolling in a graduate program) or career hopes they might have (e.g., to become administrators, or specialists at the district level).

Careful thinking about the population and behavior of interest, your own knowledge, discussion with experts and representatives of the population of interest, and review of related literature will all help you decide on the most important external variables to include in your questionnaire.

Step 6: Testing Your Questionnaire

Whenever possible, you should test your questionnaire with the kind of people you expect to complete it. Probably the most important thing you can learn from this testing is how people respond to the questionnaire. You can learn whether they find any questions unclear, confusing, irritating, or offensive. For this aspect of the testing, a group review and interview might be best, in which people are encouraged to spontaneously ask questions, make comments, and provide suggestions. Having another person help you record responses would be useful.

A further aspect of testing involves entry and analysis of the data collected during the test. This is the fullest test of whether the questionnaire is functioning as expected and gives you a final opportunity to correct any problems. You will need to read Chapter 8 for tips on data analysis before doing this, but an initial performance of some of these analyses will help you judge the validity of your measures. A good tip suggested by Michael Quinn Patton (1978) is to test an instrument by administering it to two groups known to be highly different on important measures of the instrument. For example, you might test a scale of attitude toward voting for the new bond issue with parents who have children in school versus retired people.

EFFECTIVE DATA COLLECTION

A most helpful guide to effective data collection, especially for suggestions on how to increase response rates, is Don Dillman's book *Mail and Internet Surveys: The Tailored Design Method* (2000). A review of the procedures recommended in this book will be well worth your time. Dr. Dillman is recognized internationally as a major contributor to the development of modern mail, telephone, and Internet survey methods.

CHAPTER SUMMARY

This chapter has taken you through the six steps for collecting data for your study using the MORA:

- Selecting your samples
- Eliciting outcome and normative beliefs
- Selecting beliefs common to the population
- Developing the scales for your questionnaire
- Adding questions external to the model
- Testing your questionnaire

These steps can also be applied—with modification of the belief-elicitation questions—to studying an attitude toward an object.

PART III

Understanding and Applying Your Results

Analyzing
and Reporting
Your Results

Now that you have refined your problem to a research question, developed your instrument, and collected your data—you can begin your analyses! This chapter will show you what analyses need to be done to make sense of the data and how you can best report the data. Examples of the figure and the tables you will use are included in this chapter.

You might want help to perform the data entry and analyses. If your district doesn't have a research office, help can be found in many colleges and universities. Psychology, sociology, and education departments often have experienced students who are eager to undertake outside projects for pay. You will need someone with access to a computer and a statistical analysis program such as the widely used *Statistical Package for the Social Sciences* (SPSS).

This chapter will tell you the most important analyses to have done and suggest ways you might think of others, depending on how your data turn out.

Before you perform any analyses, transform the scores on scales measuring variables in the model. This is easily done by subtracting 4 from each score on a variable of the model. Do you remember how the scale values shown in the previous examples ranged from +3 to −3? The data, however, will be entered into the statistical package as variables ranging from 1 to 7. By subtracting 4 from each score of a variable in the model, you will transform these model scales from unipolar (1 to 7) to bipolar (+3 to −3), which more clearly represent these values. (But don't subtract 4 from nonmodel items such as age or years of experience!)

One caution, however: You do *not* want to transform the "motivation to comply" scales, as they are intended to be unipolar, because few adults desire to do the exact opposite of what their "important others" think they should do. The scale below is an example of a motivation-to-comply scale.

Usually, I want to do what my family wants me to do

extremely likely ___:___:___:___:___:___:___ extremely unlikely

TWO STATISTICAL PROCEDURES USED

Two statistical procedures are needed for a study applying the model of reasoned action (MORA). Both are measures of the strength of a *linear* relationship between variables, and most statistics programs, such as SPSS, can provide them.

Correlation

The first procedure is the single correlation, symbolized by the lowercase letter *r*. (Most often this is a *Pearson's product moment* correlation.) A correlation can have a value anywhere from +1 (perfect *positive* relationship), to zero (no relationship whatsoever), to −1 (perfect *negative* relationship). The further the correlation moves from zero, and the closer it gets to +1 or −1, the stronger the relationship is between the two variables.

A positive correlation (e.g., 0.83) between the two variables X and Y indicates that when variable X goes up, variable Y also goes up, in this example, nearly as high as X. A negative correlation (e.g., -0.48) indicates an inverse relationship between two variables: When variable X goes up, variable Y goes down, but in this example, not so low as X.

In addition to reporting the strength of a correlation (e.g., $r = 0.74$), you must also report the *statistical significance* of the correlation (e.g., $p < .05$). Statistical significance can be thought of as a measure of the likelihood that the correlation's value is due to chance, rather than to an actual relationship. If the probability that the correlation's value is due to chance is less than 5% (e.g., $p < .05$), the correlation is considered *significant*.

A statistically *significant* correlation, however, is not always *important*, as the strength of the correlation must also be considered. Generally, there are a variety of guidelines for interpreting the strength of a correlation. One recent set of guidelines suggests that correlations below .30 can be considered negligible, those from .40 to .60 as moderate to strong, and those at .70 or above as strong (Charles & Mertler, 2002, p. 114).

Multiple Correlation

The second procedure is the multiple correlation, which is symbolized by an uppercase R. This procedure is similar to the single correlation, in that it measures the strength of relationship between two or more variables (e.g., attitude and norm) and a third variable (e.g., behavioral intention). The multiple correlation can have any value from zero (no relationship) to $+1$ (strongest possible relationship). In addition, this statistic gives you the *beta weights* (standardized regression coefficients) that tell you the relative importance of each of the variables (e.g., attitude and norm) used to predict a third variable (e.g., behavioral intention).

Determining the Relative Influence of Attitude and Norm

The first step is to determine the relative influence of attitude and subjective norm in forming behavioral intention. This will tell you whether you need to focus on changing the beliefs that form attitude, those that form norm, or those that form both variables. (Of course, attitude and norm might both be sufficiently important that you'll want to focus on both of them.)

To determine the relative influence of attitude and subjective norm, you perform a multiple regression, a statistical procedure that tells you how closely related two or more variables (e.g., attitude and norm) are to a third variable (e.g., behavioral intention). The "multiple R" is a measure of association, a measure of an empirical relationship between variables. This is much the same as a single correlation (r) between two variables, except that there are more variables involved.

The multiple regression will also tell you something else: the relative importance of attitude and norm in forming intention. Look at the *beta weights* (the standardized regression coefficients) produced by the regression. The size of these beta weights and their statistical significance tell you the relative influence of attitude and norm on the intentions of *your* specific group of people, concerning the behavior of interest to *you*.

Testing Your In-Common Belief Sets

The next step is to determine how well the in-common outcome and normative belief sets used in the questionnaire really captured the beliefs salient to the group you are studying.

First, add the scores on outcome belief-evaluation products to produce an indirect measure of attitude. Perform a *Pearson's product moment* correlation between this indirect measure and your direct measure of attitude toward the behavior. (See the Resources section for examples of scales and a sample questionnaire.) The higher the correlation, the better you have captured the outcome beliefs that formed the attitudes of the group you are studying.

Next, sum the scores on normative belief-motivation products to produce an indirect measure of subjective norm. Correlate this indirect measure of norm and your direct measure of norm. (See the sample questionnaire in the Resources section for examples of scales.) The higher the correlation, the more likely it is that you captured the beliefs that formed the norm of the group you are studying.

UNDERSTANDING DIFFERENCES
BETWEEN HIGH- AND LOW-INTENTION GROUPS

There are three steps to understanding the differences between intention groups.

First Step

First, obtain a frequency distribution of the intention scores of all respondents. In SPSS, the output will look like the example in Table 8.1 below. Although all these numbers might look a little intimidating at first, we will walk you through them column by column.

Look at the *Value* column. Value refers to the scale points on the intention scale, with −3 being *extremely unlikely,* 3 being *extremely likely,* and 0 being *neither likely nor unlikely.* The numeral 9 is typically used to signify missing cases (instances in which a respondent failed to respond to a given item). In this example, we have 7 missing cases.

You will notice that two rows are labeled *Total.* The first total row includes all valid cases (valid responses to the question). The second total row includes missing cases (respondents to the questionnaire, but not to the question).

Table 8.1   Facsimile of SPSS Frequency Distribution of Scores on
Intention

Value	Frequency	Percentage	Valid Percentage	Cumulative Percentage
−3	12	7.9	8.3	8.3
−2	15	9.9	10.4	18.7
−1	26	17.2	18.1	36.8
0	35	23.2	24.3	61.1
1	29	19.2	20.1	81.2
2	17	11.3	11.8	93.0
3	10	6.6	6.9	99.9[a]
Total	144	95.3	99.9[a]	
Missing	9	7	4.6	
Total	151	99.9[a]		

a. Percentage does not equal 100% due to rounding.

The second column, *Frequency,* shows you the number of respondents at each value. For example, value −3 has a frequency of 12, which means that 12 respondents stated that it was *extremely unlikely* that they would perform the behavior. Value 3 has a frequency of 10, which indicates that 10 respondents stated that it was *extremely likely* that they *would* perform the behavior. Value 0 has a frequency of 35, which means that 35 respondents stated that it was *neither likely nor unlikely* that they would perform the behavior. (These respondents just couldn't make up their minds!)

The *Percent* column shows the percentage of all responses at each value. The percentages in this column are based on the division of the frequency at each value by the total number of cases (including missing cases), in this example, 151 cases. The *Valid Percent* column shows the percentage of all responses at each value (excluding missing cases), in this example, 144 cases. The percentages in the *Valid Percent* column are those typically reported.

The *Cumulative Percentage* column gives you a running total of all percentages at each value.

Second Step

The second step to understanding the differences between intention groups is to divide your respondents into groups to see what differences in their beliefs cause the difference in their intentions. Typically, people using the model divide respondents into two groups, those who intend to perform the behavior and those who do not. In the example in Table 8.1, this would mean grouping all those with negative intention scores into one group of 53 respondents and those with positive scores into another group of 56. The 35 cases in the neutral value would be excluded from the analysis.

However, there are many ways to divide scores, depending on (a) your specific research question, (b) your sample size (it's best to have at least 60 cases), and (c) how your scores are distributed (it's best to compare groups of as nearly equal size as possible).

For example, if your sample is large enough, you might want to divide respondents into three groups: (a) those who will perform the behavior (scores of $+1$ to $+3$), (b) those who will *not* perform the behavior (scores of -1 to -3), and (c) those who are undecided (scores of 0). The undecided group (scores of 0, and perhaps -1 and $+1$) is likely to be easier to influence in the desired direction than those with more extreme scores (e.g., -3 and -2).

Third Step

The third step is to divide the respondents' scores according to your plan and compare the two groups using T^2 tests (or ANOVA) and t tests. These tests tell you whether a given between-group difference is large enough to be statistically significant. You will want to compare between-group differences on all variables, but especially:

- Intention to perform the behavior (I_B)
- Attitude toward the behavior (A_B)

- The summed outcome belief-evaluation products that form attitude (estimated A_B)
- Subjective norm
- The summed normative belief-motivation products that form subjective norm (estimated SN)
- Any external variables you measured, such as:
  - Other attitudes
  - Other behavioral intentions
  - Any behavioral variables of interest (e.g., "Did you vote in last year's bond issue?")
  - Demographic variables

To report these between-group differences, you can use a table such as Table 8.2 below. This table reports differences by intention group on most variables.

Because of their complexity, separate tables are required to report between-group differences on the outcome beliefs, evaluations, and products that form attitude, and the normative beliefs, motivations, and products that form subjective norm. Tables 8.3 and 8.4 are examples of these tables.

Understanding the Influence
of the Beliefs That Underlie Attitude

Table 8.3 reports the 15 most frequently elicited beliefs reported in Table 7.2 and how the mean scores of respondents in each of the intention groups differ on outcome beliefs, evaluations, and products. Notice how the 15 outcome beliefs are divided into three groups of five beliefs each. This division puts a little "white space" between the groups and makes the table easier to read.

Suppose that a T^2 test found significant overall differences between the two groups on evaluations and belief-evaluation products. The two groups were, however, pretty much alike in the strength and direction of their beliefs. Independent sample *t* tests compared the two groups' mean scores. To reduce the

Table 8.2 Differences in Mean Scores of High- and Low-
Intention Groups

	Intention Group		
Outcome	High (n = 53)	Low (n = 64)	t value
Intention	2.0	−1.1	16.2**
Global attitude	2.5	1.2	6.6**
Attitude toward behavior	2.4	0.7	7.0**
Estimated attitude (S be)	51.3	37.0	2.5*
Norm	2.2	1.4	3.3**
Estimated norm (S bm)	86.5	31.6	5.5**
Teaching experience at current level	5.3	4.6	0.8
Other teaching experience	2.1	4.2	−1.7
Gender (%)			
Male	19.4	32.9	NA
Female	80.6	67.1	NA
Grade level (%)			
Elementary	42.7	57.3	NA
Secondary	55.8	44.2	NA

Note: Respondents whose intention scores were positive (1–3) were grouped
as "high," and those whose scores were neutral or negative (0 through −3)
were grouped "low."

* $p < .05$

** $p < .01$

table's complexity, the values of these *t* tests are reported only
for the products, but the statistical significance of each difference is shown for beliefs and evaluations.

In addition, the outcomes are organized so that those with
the largest between-group differences (largest *t* values) are
at the top of the table, and those outcomes with the smallest
differences are at the bottom. This is a useful technique for
focusing the reader's eye on the outcome belief-evaluation
products that account for the greatest differences in the
groups' attitudes.

Table 8.3 Differences in Scores on Outcome Beliefs, Evaluations, and Products by Intention Group

Outcome	Belief		Evaluation		Product		
	High	Low	High	Low	High	Low	t value
I will miss seeing how my students grow up	1.0	2.9**	-1.7	-2.8**	-1.7	8.1**	9.8
I won't have to grade papers on weekends	2.8	2.9	2.9	1.6**	8.1	4.6**	3.4
I will get more interaction with adults	2.3	2.0	2.3	1.0**	5.3	2.0**	3.3
I won't have to grade papers at night	2.8	2.7	2.9	1.8**	8.1	4.9**	3.2
I won't have extraneous duties	2.2	2.0	2.9	1.8**	6.4	3.6*	2.8
I will meet more interesting people	1.7	0.8*	2.3	1.5**	3.9	1.2*	2.7
I will get a better paying job	2.4	1.9*	2.7	2.0*	6.5	4.0*	2.5
I will get more technical support	2.4	2.3	2.9	2.0*	7.0	4.6*	2.4
I will get a defined lunch hour	2.7	2.8	2.8	1.9*	7.6	5.3*	2.3
More intellectual stimulation	2.4	1.7*	2.6	2.3	6.2	3.9*	2.3
I won't have summers off	2.7	2.5	-2.6	-2.4	7.0	6.0	1.0
I will get a more attractive workplace	1.9	1.6	2.0	1.8	3.8	2.9	0.9
I will have to travel	2.2	2.3	2.5	2.1*	5.5	4.8	0.7
I will expand my social life	0.9	0.7	1.2	0.9	1.1	0.6	0.5
I will miss being in control of my own work	1.5	1.3	-2.2	-2.7*	-3.3	-3.5	0.2

Note: Belief and evaluation scales range from +3 (*extremely good, likely*) to –3 (*extremely bad, unlikely*) through a neutral midpoint of zero (*neither*). The size of differences between intention groups on belief-evaluation products is shown by the *t* values in the last column. Statistical significance of between-group differences on beliefs, evaluations, and belief-evaluation products is calculated by independent *t* tests, and indicated by asterisks.

* $p < .05$

** $p < .01$

Table 8.4   Differences in Scores on Normative Beliefs, Motivations, and Products by Intention Group

Normative	Belief		Motivation		Product		
	High	Low	High	Low	High	Low	t value
Family	2.5	-0.9**	5.6	5.3	14.0	-4.8**	18.8
My principal	-1.6	-2.8*	0.8	5.3**	-1.3	-14.8**	13.5
District administration	-1.3	-2.6 *	0.6	4.8*	-0.8	-12.5*	11.7
Fellow teachers	-1.1	-2.6*	1.2	4.5*	-1.3	-11.7**	10.4
Parents of students	-1.3	-2.4*	0.3	3.9*	-0.4	-9.4*	9.0
My students	-0.6	-2.1**	2.0	3.8*	-1.2	-8.0*	6.8
My school board	-0.9	-1.4	0.5	3.7	-0.5	-5.2	4.7

Note: Normative belief scales range from +3 (*extremely likely*) to −3 (*extremely likely*) to 0 (*not at all likely*). Motivation scores range from 6 (*extremely unlikely*). The size of differences between intention groups on belief-evaluation products is shown by the *t* values in the last column. Statistical significance of between-group differences on beliefs, evaluations, and belief-evaluation products is calculated by independent *t* tests, and indicated by asterisks.

* *p* < .05

** *p* < .01

What Are the Beliefs That Underlie Attitude Toward Resigning From a School (or From Teaching)?

- Some teachers will greatly miss seeing their students grow up and hold the belief that leaving their school or field will affect this outcome.
- Table 8.3 shows the difference between high and low intenders' (intending to leave a school or field) beliefs and evaluations of not seeing students grow up.
- Notice that a very strong difference exists between high and low intenders on the evaluation strength of missing seeing their students grow up.
- Note the difference between low intenders and high intenders. Here you can see that you might want to let high intender teachers know that students will miss them! This knowledge might narrow the difference between low and high intenders.
- What else could you do once you identify how much of a difference exists on high and low intenders on a particular item?

UNDERSTANDING THE INFLUENCE OF THE BELIEFS THAT UNDERLIE NORM

Table 8.4 reports the between-group differences in mean scores on beliefs that seven referents want the teachers to resign, and in mean scores on motivation to comply with each referent. Suppose that a T^2 test found significant differences between the two groups on beliefs, motivations, and belief-motivation products.

Independent sample t tests compared the mean scores of two groups. To reduce the table's complexity, the values of these t tests are reported only for products, but the statistical significance of differences is indicated throughout by asterisks.

The normative beliefs are organized so that those with the largest between-group differences are at the top of the table, and those with the smallest differences are at the bottom. This is a useful technique for focusing the reader's eye on the normative belief-motivation products that cause the largest differences in the groups' norms.

Figures often illustrate concepts and relationships better than words and numbers alone. Figure 8.1 illustrates the model's variables of behavioral intention, attitude toward the behavior, outcome beliefs and evaluations, subjective norm, and normative beliefs and motivation to comply. In contrast with Figure 5.1, Figure 8.1 reports hypothetical study data.

The strength and significance of correlations are shown between (a) outcome belief-evaluation products (estimated attitude) and attitude, and (b) normative belief-motivation products (estimated subjective norm). These figures tell how well your belief elicitation and analysis captured the same beliefs that were salient for your population when

Figure 8.1   Hypothetical Results From Applying the Model of Reasoned Action

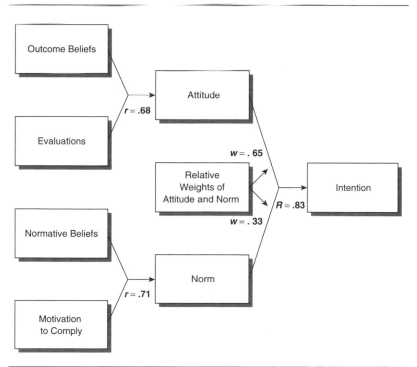

you administered the final questionnaire. The strength of the multiple correlation between (a) attitude and norm and (b) intention shows how strongly those variables were related to intention. The beta weights show the relative importance of attitude and norm in forming intention.

Chapter Summary

In this chapter, we have covered the essential steps in analyzing and reporting your results. Once you complete the analyses discussed above and share the results with relevant audiences, you might find further analyses you would like to do. For example, you might want to look at other differences among your respondents according to certain background variables.

- Do principals in site-based, decision-making schools evaluate outcomes differently from other principals?
- Are there differences in the attitudes or beliefs on an issue between teachers from traditional teacher preparation programs and teachers from postbaccalaureate programs?
- Do teachers with five years of experience evaluate outcomes differently than new teachers?
- Do first-year assistant principals have different perceptions of social pressure than experienced principals?
- Are parents with more than one child in school more likely to volunteer in school activities than parents with only one child?
- Do teachers whose students have shown significant improvement in standardized test scores have different beliefs and evaluations than those whose students have not shown such improvements?
- In what ways do central office administrators (e.g., curriculum director) differ from school principals in beliefs or evaluations of outcomes?

Applying
Your Results
to Your Interest

School leaders have many problems to solve and many opportunities to achieve. Although these concerns are varied, many of them can be resolved more effectively by using the model of reasoned action. Examples of these concerns include understanding why voters will or will not support a bond issue, why parents do or do not participate in education, and why teachers remain in school or resign from teaching.

The problem of teacher attrition is a serious one, especially in schools and districts that are underfunded. Let us look, therefore, at an example of a principal using the model to enhance teacher retention. The data and other information in this chapter illustrate one use of the model and one type of results. Your applications of the model are likely to differ in many, or all, respects.

Imagine that you are the principal of River High School, a large campus that brings together students from diverse backgrounds and experiences. Your school's teachers are a diverse group as well. Many are happy in their chosen profession (low intenders), but others are thinking about resigning from teaching to seek employment outside education (high intenders).

By applying the model of reasoned action (MORA), you will learn what can be done to influence teachers who intend to resign (high intenders). After collecting and entering your data into a computerized software program, you are ready to analyze your results and see what can be done to influence intentions in a *negative* direction (i.e., *against* resigning).

WHICH IS MORE IMPORTANT: ATTITUDE OR NORM?

The first thing you ought to do is learn whether you must influence favorable attitudes toward resigning or perceptions of social pressure (subjective norm) to resign. To find out the relative importance of attitude and subjective norm, you regress the measure of intention on measures of attitude and norm. You discover that attitude has a significant beta weight (standardized regression coefficient) of .654 ($p < .01$). You discover that subjective norm has a significant beta weight of .325 ($p < .01$). This means that in this situation, *both* attitude and norm are important influences on your teachers' intentions, but that attitude is the more important of the two.

Your best chance of influencing intentions in a direction *against* resigning will be to influence, to the degree possible, both attitude and norm. Let us first examine attitude formation and change and then look at formation and change of subjective norm.

FORMATION OF FAVORABLE ATTITUDE TOWARD RESIGNING FROM TEACHING

As some of the teachers think about resigning from teaching, they automatically begin thinking about a number of likely outcomes, as reported in Table 9.1. They perceive some of these outcomes as quite likely to follow their resignation, such as not having to grade papers at night or on the weekend,

Table 9.1   Differences in Scores on Outcome Beliefs, Evaluations, and Products by Intention Group

Outcome	Belief		Evaluation		Product		t value
	High	Low	High	Low	High	Low	
I will miss seeing how my students grow up	1.0	2.9**	-1.7	-2.8**	-1.7	8.1**	9.8
I won't have to grade papers on weekends	2.8	2.9	2.9	1.6**	8.1	4.6**	3.4
I will get more interaction with adults	2.3	2.0	2.3	1.0**	5.3	2.0**	3.3
I won't have to grade papers at night	2.8	2.7	2.9	1.8**	8.1	4.9**	3.2
I won't have extraneous duties	2.2	2.0	2.9	1.8**	6.4	3.6*	2.8
I will meet more interesting people	1.7	0.8*	2.3	1.5**	3.9	1.2*	2.7
I will get a better paying job	2.4	1.9*	2.7	2.0*	6.5	4.0*	2.5
I will get more technical support	2.4	2.3	2.9	2.0*	7.0	4.6*	2.4
I will get a defined lunch hour	2.7	2.8	2.8	1.9*	7.6	5.3*	2.3
More intellectual stimulation	2.4	1.7*	2.6	2.3	6.2	3.9*	2.3
I won't have summers off	2.7	2.5	-2.6	-2.4	7.0	6.0	1.0
I will get a more attractive workplace	1.9	1.6	2.0	1.8	3.8	2.9	0.9
I will have to travel	2.2	2.3	2.5	2.1*	5.5	4.8	0.7
I will expand my social life	0.9	0.7	1.2	0.9	1.1	0.6	0.5
I will miss being in control of my own work	1.5	1.3	-2.2	-2.7*	-3.3	-3.5	0.2

Note: Belief and evaluation scales range from +3 (*extremely good, likely*) through a neutral midpoint of zero (*neither*) to -3 (*extremely bad, unlikely*). The size of differences between intention groups on belief-evaluation products is shown by the *t* values in the last column. Statistical significance of between-group differences on beliefs, evaluations, and belief-evaluation products is calculated by independent *t* tests, and indicated by asterisks.

* $p < .05$

** $p < .01$

and that a new job would require that they work during the summer. Other outcomes are seen as somewhat less likely, such as resignation expanding their social lives. Some of these outcomes they evaluate favorably, and others they do not.

This table makes clear what the differences are, between high and low intenders, in the formation of their attitudes toward resigning. You want to look for differences in the following three areas:

- The strength and direction of their beliefs in the likelihood of outcomes following resignation
- The strength and direction of their evaluations of these outcomes
- The belief-evaluation products that form attitude toward the behavior

The differences in their beliefs and evaluations (in this example, differences are mostly on evaluations) determine what between-group differences there will be on belief-evaluation products. It is these belief-evaluation products that form attitude—which is the more important component of intention—in this example. To influence attitude in a negative direction (*against* resigning), you will need to influence the beliefs or evaluations of the teachers who intend to resign.

If *you* were the principal, and you saw Table 9.1, what would you do to influence the high-intention teachers' attitudes in the desired direction, that is, toward a *negative* attitude toward resigning?

CHANGE OF ATTITUDE TO OPPOSE RESIGNING FROM TEACHING

First Way to Change Attitude

Here we have a favorable attitude toward resigning that the principal would like to change to an unfavorable attitude. The first way to change attitude in an *unfavorable direction* is to *reduce the strength of one or more of the positively evaluated outcomes.*

One of the most favorably evaluated outcomes of resigning to seek other employment is "More intellectual stimulation." Both high- and low-intention groups evaluate this positively, but the high intenders believe it a more likely outcome of resigning than do the low intenders.

Knowing this, the principal could negotiate the development of a site-based master's program with the local state university. Most classes could be taught in the district's professional development center, and teachers could take courses while keeping their jobs. Either or both of these items of information could significantly reduce or eliminate teachers' beliefs that resigning would bring them more intellectual stimulation than staying in teaching.

The principal could also negotiate with the district to have it pay a portion of the tuition for district teachers enrolled in the program. When teachers are informed of this program, it is likely that many will no longer believe—or at least not believe so strongly—that they will obtain *more* intellectual stimulation by resigning than by remaining at River High School.

Another outcome of resigning that is favorably evaluated by both groups is "won't have extraneous duties." The high intenders evaluate this much more favorably than the low intenders, but both groups believe it with about the same strength.

What could a principal do with this information?

One response would be for the principal to develop a Teacher Assistance Program (TAP). The TAP would perform duties that are extraneous to teaching, such as lunchroom duty, hall duty, bus duty, and other duties. The TAP participants would include recently retired teachers, other retirees, and parents in the community. Some of these participants might be on the district payroll, paid for out of grant funds, while others might be volunteers.

Second Way to Change Attitude

The second way to change attitude in a *negative* or *unfavorable direction* is to *strengthen beliefs in negatively evaluated outcomes.* There are only three of these in this example, "miss seeing how students grow up," "not have summers off," and "miss control of my own work." Both intention groups quite negatively evaluate the last outcome, but it is not very strongly held by either group. There are a number of possibilities for strengthening beliefs in this very negatively viewed outcome.

One possibility would be for the principal to use a videotaped dramatization introducing students to the business world. This would show the high school students what they could expect in the way of working conditions, whether they seek jobs immediately, after high school graduation, or after college graduation.

One of the purposes of the videotape would be to demonstrate to students that a person's autonomy is somewhat greater at each level of education. It would, however, point out that even most college graduates report to a supervisor and expect direct supervision in their work. The principal could show the videotape at all department faculty meetings for the teachers' review and comment before student viewing.

It is likely that this reminder of what working conditions are like in the business world would strengthen teachers' beliefs that resigning to look for employment outside education would result in their missing control of their own work.

Another possibility would be for the principal to schedule a faculty meeting to get teacher input on the desirability of block scheduling and flextime. The principal might remind the faculty members that "Although in the business world schedules are usually set by the top administrators to suit production, in education we view teachers as professionals who should have a voice in when, and how, they work."

Instead of meeting a class five days a week for 50 minutes a day, teachers might meet a class for two and a half hours, twice a week. Teachers might well favor this approach as it involves less grading, more hands-on work, and more student-generated activities. These efforts might well move attitude toward resigning in a noticeably less favorable direction.

But there is more work yet to be done.

Third Way to Change Attitude

The third way to change attitude in an *unfavorable direction* is to *add new beliefs* about outcomes that will be *unfavorably* or *negatively* evaluated to the salient set of outcome beliefs. Once you know how a group evaluates one set of outcomes, it becomes much easier to imagine what *additional* outcomes would be negatively evaluated.

For example, one message might say, "If you leave teaching, all the work you've put into planning lessons, and all your experience, will be lost." Teachers might also be told, "If you leave teaching, you might miss your place as a valued professional in the community."

Another example is that given the teachers' highly *unfavorable* evaluations of losing their autonomy, perhaps school policies and procedures could be changed in ways to increase teacher autonomy. The possibilities would largely depend on existing district and school policies, but the following three ideas suggest what might be done.

One possibility would be to revise policy on supplies, so that teachers would no longer have to ask a staff worker for what they need. A second possibility would be to revise policies on arrival and departure times, so that teachers sign in and out of campus each day, but the times are not monitored. A third possibility would be to revise policies on describing the reason for personal or sick days taken off.

The creation of an on-site master's degree program would likely create—through inference processes—a number of new beliefs among the teachers about outcomes of resigning that would be negatively evaluated. These might include the idea that resigning would result in their losing many outcomes of remaining at the school and enrolling in the new master's program. These might also include new and attractive responsibilities and perhaps a new job that would follow completion of the master's program. Teachers might also infer that enrolling in the master's program would result in their "meeting interesting people."

FORMATION OF NORM TO FAVOR RESIGNING FROM TEACHING

We have seen in Chapter 4 how subjective norm is formed. Beliefs that certain persons or groups want us to behave a certain way and our motivation to comply with each person or group form our perception of social pressure regarding the behavior. To continue with our example, suppose the two intention groups have the normative beliefs, motivations, and products shown in Table 9.2.

The groups differ overall on normative beliefs, motivations, and products.

Now, how would you (as principal) go about influencing the norms of the high intention group in a negative way, so as to oppose their resigning?

CHANGE OF NORM TO OPPOSE RESIGNING FROM TEACHING

It seems just about as likely that school leaders will want to prevent behaviors (e.g., teachers resigning, students dropping out) as it does that they will want to promote behaviors (e.g., teachers integrating technology, students taking more advanced placement courses). The behavior of interest here (resigning from teaching) is *not* desired by the principal. This means that the three ways of influencing norm discussed earlier (in Chapter 4) are just the opposite from when the behavior is desired.

Changes in beliefs about outcomes of a behavior can change beliefs about the behavioral expectations of important others. In our example, the principal's initiative in collaborating with the local state university to create an on-site master's program influenced not only teachers' attitudes toward resigning but also their perceptions of social pressure to resign. Other teachers might ask them to stay and join the master's cohort.

Table 9.2 Differences in Scores on Normative Beliefs, Motivations, and Products by Intention Group

Normative	Belief		Motivation		Product		
	High	*Low*	*High*	*Low*	*High*	*Low*	*t value*
Family	2.5	-0.9**	5.6	5.3	14.0	-4.8**	18.8
My principal	-1.6	-2.8*	0.8	5.3**	-1.3	-14.8**	13.5
District administration	-1.3	-2.6*	0.6	4.8*	-0.8	-12.5*	11.7
Fellow teachers	-1.1	-2.6*	1.2	4.5*	-1.3	-11.7**	10.4
Parents of students	-1.3	-2.4*	0.3	3.9*	-0.4	-9.4*	9.0
My students	-0.6	-2.1**	2.0	3.8*	-1.2	-8.0*	6.8
My school board	-0.9	-1.4	0.5	3.7	-0.5	-5.2	4.7

Note: Normative belief scales range from +3 (*extremely likely*) to −3 (*extremely likely*) to 0 (*not at all likely*). Motivation scores range from 6 (*extremely likely*) to 0 (*not at all likely*). The size of differences between intention groups on belief-evaluation products is shown by the *t* values in the last column. Statistical significance of between-group differences on beliefs, evaluations, and belief-evaluation products is calculated by independent *t* tests, and indicated by asterisks.

* *p* < .05

** *p* < .01

First Way to Change Norm

In this example, the *first* way focuses on *negative* referents, that is, those people or groups who are perceived as *opposing* the performance of a desired behavior. This way attempts to *increase* the strength of these normative beliefs. (You must increase strength of beliefs that referents do *not* want your population to perform the behavior.)

The opportunity to earn a master's degree and the enhancement this would bring to classroom instruction might well reduce the strength of teachers' beliefs that a variety of other referents would want them to resign, including the following:

- The principal
- Students
- Parents of students
- The district administration

Second Way to Change Norm

The *second* way focuses on *positive* referents, that is, those people or groups seen as *favoring* the performance of the behavior. This way attempts to *decrease* the strength of normative beliefs. (You must reduce the strength of beliefs that referents want your population to perform the behavior.)

The opportunity to earn a master's degree, with part of the tuition paid by the district, and the opportunities and increased salary made possible by the degree might very well significantly reduce the strength of high-intention teachers' beliefs that their families want them to resign.

Third Way to Change Norm

The *third* way is to add new referents to the salient normative belief set. In our example, this way attempts to add referents who would *oppose* the behavior. (You must add beliefs about new referents who do *not* want your population to perform the behavior.) Some of the referents who might be seen as *not* wanting the teachers to resign would include the following:

- The local university's college of education, from which many of the teachers were graduated
- The district curriculum director
- The local teachers association

CHAPTER SUMMARY

In this chapter, we have seen a few examples of how a school leader might influence attitudes, norms, and intentions in a desired direction. Your school will present interesting new challenges. What intentions would you like to influence?

Resource A

Glossary of Key Terms[*]

Conceptual and Operational Definitions of Key Terms

Term	Definition	
	Conceptual	*Operational*
Belief	A thought linking an attribute with an object or a person with performance of a behavior	A point on a bipolar probability scale
Attitude	A positive, negative, or neutral affect toward some object	A point on a bipolar evaluative scale
Subjective Norm	An inferred perception about the behavioral expectations of one's "important others"	A point on a bipolar normative (probability) scale
Intention	A special kind of belief that links a person with his performance of a behavior	A point on a bipolar intention (probability) scale
Behavior	An overt, observable act, studied in its own right	Can be operationalized as a dichotomous or continuous variable

[*]Adapted with permission from the participants' manual for the workshop *Have You Got Attitude?: Understanding, & Changing Motivation, & Behavior,* last presented at the meeting of the American Evaluation Association, November 2001, St. Louis, MO.

Resource B

Sample Scales

Common Attitude Scales

Guilford Self-Rating Scale (Traditional Format)

My attitude toward technology

favorable _____:_____:_____:_____:_____:_____:_____ unfavorable
　　　　　extremely　quite　slightly　neither　slightly　quite　extremely

Guilford Self-Rating Scale (Modified Traditional Format)

My attitude toward technology

extremely favorable ____:____:____:____:____:____:____ extremely unfavorable

Guilford Self-Rating Scale (Numeric Format)

My attitude toward technology

extremely favorable　7　6　5　4　3　2　1　extremely unfavorable

Semantic Differential Scale (Traditional Format)

Technology is

good _____:_____:_____:_____:_____:_____:_____ bad
　　　　extremely　quite　slightly　neither　slightly　quite　extremely

foolish _____:_____:_____:_____:_____:_____:_____ wise
　　　　extremely　quite　slightly　neither　slightly　quite　extremely

timely _____:_____:_____:_____:_____:_____:_____ untimely
　　　　extremely　quite　slightly　neither　slightly　quite　extremely

wasteful _____:_____:_____:_____:_____:_____:_____ thrifty
　　　　extremely　quite　slightly　neither　slightly　quite　extremely

Scales of Other Model Variables

Intention

I will resign my teaching position next semester to seek other employment

extremely likely 7   6   5   4   3   2   1 extremely unlikely

Attitude

My attitude toward resigning my teaching position next semester to seek other employment is

extremely favorable 7   6   5   4   3   2   1 extremely unfavorable

Outcome Belief

Resigning my teaching position next semester to seek other employment will result in a less stressful workplace for me

extremely likely 7   6   5   4   3   2   1 extremely unlikely

Outcome Evaluation

A less stressful workplace for me is

extremely good 7   6   5   4   3   2   1 extremely bad

Subjective Norm (Traditional)

Most people or groups who are important to *me* think I should resign my teaching position next semester to seek other employment

extremely likely 7   6   5   4   3   2   1   extremely unlikely

Subjective Norm (Modified)

Most people or groups who are important to *my career* think I should resign my teaching position next semester to seek other employment

extremely likely 7   6   5   4   3   2   1   extremely unlikely

Note: Emphasis added here to highlight differences in the two normative measures.

Normative Belief

My spouse thinks I should resign my teaching position next semester to seek other employment

extremely likely 7   6   5   4   3   2   1   extremely unlikely

Motivation to Comply

Generally, I want to do what my spouse wants me to do

extremely likely 7   6   5   4   3   2   1   extremely unlikely

---

SOURCE: Adapted with permission from the participants' manual for the workshop *Have You Got Attitude?: Understanding and Changing Motivation and Behavior,* last presented at the meeting of the American Evaluation Association, November 2001, St. Louis, MO.

Resource C

Sample Questionnaire

(Question types, etc. are indicated in **Arial Black** font)

Date

Teacher Feedback Form

Instructions

In responding to the following questions, consider a networked multimedia computer (with CD-ROM drive) connected to the Internet as the technology that you will integrate, **if** you choose to integrate technology into your teaching.

These questions ask you to either (a) rate things on their degree of likelihood (*likely, unlikely*) or (b) to evaluate them (*good/bad*). **The midpoint of each scale ("4") should be used if** you are *unsure* how to rate the item (e.g., "Don't know"), or if you are neutral (e.g., "I don't really agree or disagree").

The numbers from 7 to 5 are likely or favorable (e.g., extremely likely, quite likely, slightly likely; extremely good, quite good, slightly good), the numbers from 3 to 1 are **un**likely or **un**favorable or bad. For example:

likely/good   *unlikely/bad*

extremely	quite	slightly	neither	slightly	quite	extremely
7	6	5	4	3	2	1

Circle the number closest to your opinion

Distractor questions (used to minimize social desirability bias)

Preferences

1. My integrating a multimedia computer into my teaching would significantly enhance student learning

   extremely likely   7   6   5   4   3   2   1   extremely unlikely

2. I like the idea of integrating the multimedia computer into my teaching by the 2004–2005 school year

   extremely likely   7   6   5   4   3   2   1   extremely unlikely

Background questions (typically put at the end, but these fit in context)

Hard Reality

3. My level of expertise in using a multimedia computer

   extremely high   7   6   5   4   3   2   1   extremely low

4. My level of expertise in integrating a multimedia computer into my teaching

   extremely high   7   6   5   4   3   2   1   extremely low

5. I *currently* have sufficient access to the resources I would *need* to integrate a multimedia computer into my teaching

   extremely likely   7   6   5   4   3   2   1   extremely unlikely

Intention

6. I will integrate the multimedia computer into my teaching by the 2004–2005 school year

   extremely likely   7   6   5   4   3   2   1   extremely unlikely

Attitude toward behavior

7. My attitude toward (feeling about) integrating the multi-media computer into my teaching by the 2004–2005 school year

   extremely favorable 7 6 5 4 3 2 1 extremely unfavorable

Outcome evaluations

Please evaluate the following:

8. My having to deal with technology problems

   extremely good 7   6   5   4   3   2   1 extremely bad

9. Quick access to a wealth of information

   extremely good 7   6   5   4   3   2   1 extremely bad

10. Keeping kids on task and finding ways to share too few computers

    extremely good 7   6   5   4   3   2   1 extremely bad

11. All students becoming computer literate

    extremely good 7   6   5   4   3   2   1 extremely bad

12. A good resource for lesson planning

    extremely good 7   6   5   4   3   2   1 extremely bad

13. My having to find time in my teaching day to integrate technology into my teaching

    extremely good 7   6   5   4   3   2   1 extremely bad

14. My having to find time for training to become proficient in technology integration

    extremely good 7   6   5   4   3   2   1 extremely bad

15. My having to find the money for technology

    extremely good 7   6   5   4   3   2   1 extremely bad

16. Increased student motivation

    extremely good   7   6   5   4   3   2   1   extremely bad

17. Reduced student interaction

    extremely good   7   6   5   4   3   2   1   extremely bad

18. Improved student problem solving

    extremely good   7   6   5   4   3   2   1   extremely bad

19. Students directing their own learning at their own pace

    extremely good   7   6   5   4   3   2   1   extremely bad

20. Students spending too much time on computers and neglecting their assignments

    extremely good   7   6   5   4   3   2   1   extremely bad

21. Students being better prepared for jobs

    extremely good   7   6   5   4   3   2   1   extremely bad

22. Making my record keeping easier

    extremely good   7   6   5   4   3   2   1   extremely bad

23. Access to current information

    extremely good   7   6   5   4   3   2   1   extremely bad

24. Students communicating around the world

    extremely good   7   6   5   4   3   2   1   extremely bad

Outcome beliefs

How likely are the following to result from your integrating the computer into your teaching by the 2004–2005 school year?

25. My having to deal with technology problems

    extremely likely   7   6   5   4   3   2   1   extremely unlikely

26. Quick access to a wealth of information

    extremely likely   7   6   5   4   3   2   1   extremely unlikely

27. Having to keep kids on task and find ways to share too few computers

    extremely likely   7   6   5   4   3   2   1   extremely unlikely

28. All students will become computer literate

    extremely likely   7   6   5   4   3   2   1   extremely unlikely

29. A good resource for lesson planning

    extremely likely   7   6   5   4   3   2   1   extremely unlikely

30. Finding the time in my teaching day to integrate technology

    extremely likely   7   6   5   4   3   2   1   extremely unlikely

31. My finding time for training to become proficient

    extremely likely   7   6   5   4   3   2   1   extremely unlikely

32. Finding the money for technology

    extremely likely   7   6   5   4   3   2   1   extremely unlikely

33. Increased student motivation

    extremely likely   7   6   5   4   3   2   1   extremely unlikely

34. Reduction in student interaction

    extremely likely   7   6   5   4   3   2   1   extremely unlikely

35. Improved student problem solving

    extremely likely   7   6   5   4   3   2   1   extremely unlikely

36. Students direct their own learning at their own pace

    extremely likely   7   6   5   4   3   2   1   extremely unlikely

37. Students spending too much time on computers and neglecting their assignments

    extremely likely   7   6   5   4   3   2   1   extremely unlikely

38. Students being better prepared for jobs

    extremely likely   7   6   5   4   3   2   1   extremely unlikely

39. Making my record keeping easier

    extremely likely   7   6   5   4   3   2   1   extremely unlikely

40. Access to current information

    extremely likely   7   6   5   4   3   2   1   extremely unlikely

41. My students communicating around the world

    extremely likely   7   6   5   4   3   2   1   extremely unlikely

Subjective norm

42. Most people or groups who are important to me would *favor* my integrating the multimedia computer into my teaching by the 2004–2005 school year

    extremely likely   7   6   5   4   3   2   1   extremely unlikely

Motivation to comply

I generally want to do what . . .

43. My district administration thinks I should do

    extremely likely   7   6   5   4   3   2   1   extremely unlikely

44. My family thinks I should do

    extremely likely   7   6   5   4   3   2   1   extremely unlikely

45. Students' parents think I should do

    extremely likely   7   6   5   4   3   2   1   extremely unlikely

46. My building administration thinks I should do

    extremely likely   7   6   5   4   3   2   1   extremely unlikely

47. Students think I should do

    extremely likely   7   6   5   4   3   2   1   extremely unlikely

48. The community thinks I should do

    extremely likely   7   6   5   4   3   2   1   extremely unlikely

49. Other teachers think I should do

    extremely likely   7   6   5   4   3   2   1   extremely unlikely

50. The business community thinks I should do

    extremely likely   7   6   5   4   3   2   1   extremely unlikely

51. My school board thinks I should do

    extremely likely   7   6   5   4   3   2   1   extremely unlikely

Normative beliefs

52. My district administration thinks I should integrate the multimedia computer into my teaching by the 2004–2005 school year

    extremely likely   7   6   5   4   3   2   1   extremely unlikely

53. My family thinks I should integrate the multimedia computer into my teaching by the 2004–2005 school year

    extremely likely   7   6   5   4   3   2   1   extremely unlikely

54. My students' parents think I should integrate the multimedia computer into my teaching by the 2004–2005 school year

    extremely likely   7   6   5   4   3   2   1   extremely unlikely

55. My building administration thinks I should integrate the multimedia computer into my teaching by the 2004–2005 school year

    extremely likely   7   6   5   4   3   2   1   extremely unlikely

56. My students think I should integrate the multimedia computer into my teaching by the 2004–2005 school year

    extremely likely   7   6   5   4   3   2   1   extremely unlikely

57. The community thinks I should integrate the multimedia computer into my teaching by the 2004–2005 school year

    extremely likely   7   6   5   4   3   2   1   extremely unlikely

58. Other teachers think I should integrate the multimedia computer into my teaching by the 2004–2005 school year

    extremely likely   7   6   5   4   3   2   1   extremely unlikely

59. The business community thinks I should integrate the multimedia computer into my teaching by the 2004–2005 school year

    extremely likely   7   6   5   4   3   2   1   extremely unlikely

60. My school board thinks I should integrate the multimedia computer into my teaching by the 2004–2005 school year

    extremely likely   7   6   5   4   3   2   1   extremely unlikely

61. What number comes closest to indicating my *current* stage of technology use?

7	6	5	4	3	2	1
refinement	expansion	integration	infusion	exploration	awareness	nonuse

Perceived behavioral control (measures the perceived volitionality of the behavior)

62. If I *really* wanted to, I could integrate the multimedia computer into my teaching by the 2004–2005 school year

    extremely likely   7   6   5   4   3   2   1   extremely unlikely

Background question

63. My principal's regular evaluation of my teaching emphasizes my use of technology

    extremely likely   7   6   5   4   3   2   1   extremely unlikely

Qualitative question

64. If you intend to integrate the computer, please describe in a sentence or two, how you would do this:

_____

_____

_____

Background questions

Finally, just to help us analyze the data. . .

65. Gender: Male _____ Female _____

66. Years of full-time teaching experience at current level _____
at other levels _____

67. Grade(s) currently taught _____

68. Subject(s) taught _____

69. Current highest degree _____

70. I currently have tenure: _____ Yes _____ No

Thank you for your participation!

SOURCE: Adapted with permission from the participants' manual for the workshop *Have You Got Attitude?: Understanding, and Changing Motivation and Behavior,* last presented at the meeting of the American Evaluation Association, November 2001, St. Louis, MO.

Resource D

*Action Plan Checklist for a Study
Using the Model*

Task Areas

1. Research question and procedures
   1.1. Review literature if needed
   1.2. Refine research question
   1.3. Decide on population, sampling procedures, mailing procedures (e.g., number of waves of mailings, mailing dates)
   1.4. Decide on audience(s) for reporting results (see 6.2.b, 6.3)
   1.5. Draft cover letters and postcard prompt

2. Belief elicitation
   2.1. Select samples for mail instruments and telephone interviews
   2.2. Prepare and send cover letters and instruments
   2.3. Conduct telephone interviews
   2.4. Content analyze data, construct modal salient belief sets (attitude and norm)
   2.5. If belief elicitation is low, or if there is low variance on intention measure, revise focus of intention frame of reference, and repeat tasks 2.2 thru 2.4

3. Pilot study
   3.1. Prepare instrument and do in-person pretesting of instrument and cover letters; revise as needed

3.2. Select sample for pilot

3.3. Send revised instrument and First Wave cover letter

3.4. Data handling

    a. Check for questionable response patterns (e.g., all neutral, all negative)

    b. Code, input, and clean data

    c. Statistical procedures, especially item analysis of semantic differential attitude scale (see Task 5 that follows for detail)

3.5. Revise instrument, as needed, and print

4. Data collection (adopted from Dillman, 1978)

    4.1. Prepare and send First Wave cover letter and instrument (Week 1)

    4.2. Send prompt card (Week 2)

    4.3. Review and record responses, revise Second Wave cover letter and instrument if needed

    4.4. Prepare and send Second Wave cover letter and instrument (Week 4)

    4.5. Prepare and send Third Wave cover letter and instrument (Week 6)

5. Data handling and analysis

    5.1. Code, input, and clean data

    5.2. Analyze reliability and validity of instrument

    5.3. Regress intention on attitude and norm, direct and estimated measures

    5.4. Correlate direct and estimated measures of attitude and norm

    5.5. Get frequency distribution of intention scores; divide subjects into groups for analysis (e.g., "high and low intenders" or "high, medium, and low intenders")

    5.6. Examine differences in the groups' mean scores on all study variables:

        a. Overall—T^2 test on
- Outcome beliefs
- Outcome evaluations

- Outcome belief-evaluation products
- Normative beliefs
- Motivations to comply
- Normative belief-motivation products

b. Items—*t*-test on the following:
- Intention
- Attitude: direct and estimated measures
- Norm: direct and estimated measures
- Outcome beliefs, evaluations, and products
- Normative beliefs, motivation, and products
- Variables peripheral to the model (e.g., "perceived behavioral control")
- Demographic and other variables external to the model

5.7. Correlate intention, attitude, and norm with other variables

5.8. Other analyses (as suggested by these results)

6. Reporting
6.1. Full report
6.2. Abstract/summary (i.e., for public, study respondents, etc.)
6.3. Articles

NOTE: This is the most complete list of tasks we could think of. Not all tasks need be done in each study.

SOURCE: Adapted with permission from the participants' manual for the workshop *Have You Got "Attitude"?: Measuring, Attitude Understanding, and Changing and Behavior*, last presented at the meeting of the American Evaluation Association, November 2001, St. Louis, MO.

Resource E

Internet-Based Resources

Guides and Help Sites

American Psychological Association Style Guide
http://www.apastyle.org/

American Psychological Association style for electronic references
http://www.apastyle.org/elecref.html

A Guide to Grammar and Writing
http://webster.commnet.edu/grammar/index.htm

A Guide to Writing APA Style Papers
http://webster.commnet.edu/apa/apa_index.htm

Bill Trochim's Center for Social Research Methods and Knowledge Base
www.socialresearchmethods.net

Bill Trochim's Selecting Statistics Knowledge Base
www.socialresearchmethods.net

Roert Niles' Journalism Help: Statistics Every Writer Should Know
http://www.robertniles.com/stats/

Organizations

American Educational Research Association
http://www.aera.net/American Evaluation Association
http://www.eval.org/

National Council of Professors of Educational Administration
http://www.ncpea.net/

Southwest Educational Research Association
http://www.sera-edresearch.org/

References

Ajzen, I., & Fishbein, M. (1980). *Understanding attitudes and predicting social behavior.* Englewood Cliffs, NJ: Prentice Hall.

Ballone, L. M., & Czerniak, C. M. (2001). Teachers' beliefs about accommodating students' learning styles in science classes. *Electronic Journal of Science Education, 6*(2), 1–41. Retrieved from http://unr.edu/homepage/crowther/ejse/balloneetal.pdf.

Bamberg, S., & Schmidt, P. (2001). Theory-driven, subgroup-specific evaluation of an intervention to reduce private car use. *Journal of Applied Social Psychology, 31,* 1300–1329.

Bamberg, S., & Schmidt, P. (2003). Incentive, morality or habit? Predicting students' car use for university routes with the models of Ajzen, Schwartz, and Triandis. *Environment and Behavior, 35,* 1–22.

Barth, R. S. (2003). *Lessons learned: Shaping relationships and the culture of the workplace.* Thousand Oaks, CA: Corwin.

Black, S. (2001). Morale matters: When teachers feel good about their work, research shows, student achievement rises. *American School Board Journal, 188*(1), 40–43.

Bruner, D. Y., & Greenlee, B. J. (2000). Measures of work culture in high and low performing schools. *Research in the Schools, 7*(2), 71–76.

Charles, C. M., & Mertler, C. A. (2002). *Introduction to educational research* (4th ed.). Boston: Allyn & Bacon/Longman.

D'Amico, J. J., & Nelson, V. (2000). How on Earth did you hear about us? A study of exemplary rural school practices in the Upper Midwest. *Journal of Research in Rural Education, 16*(3), 182–192.

Darling-Hammond, L. (2003). Keeping good teachers: Why it matters what leaders can do. *Educational Leadership, 60*(8), 7–13.

Dillman, D.A. (2000). *Mail and Internet surveys: The tailored design method.* Indianapolis, IN: Wiley.

Fishbein, M. (1963). An investigation of the relationships between beliefs about an object and the attitude toward that object. *Human Relations, 16,* 233–240.

Fishbein, M. (Ed.). (1967). *Readings in attitude theory and measurement.* New York: John Wiley.

Fishbein, M. (1982). Social psychological analysis of smoking behavior. In J. R. Eiser (Ed.), *Social psychology and behavioral medicine* (pp. 179–197). New York: John Wiley.

Fishbein, M., & Ajzen, I. (1975). *Belief, attitude, intention, and behavior: An introduction to theory and research.* Reading, MA: Addison-Wesley.

Fullan, M. G. (2001). *The new meaning of educational change* (3rd ed.). New York: Teachers College Press.

Goodlad, J. I. (2004). *A place called school.* Boston: McGraw-Hill. (20th anniversary reissue of the 1984 edition).

Hall, G. E., & Hord, S. M. (2001). *Implementing change: Patterns, principles, and potholes.* Needham Heights, MA: Allyn & Bacon.

Hord, S. M., Rutherford, W. L., Huling-Austin, L., & Hall, G. E. (1987). *Taking charge of change.* Alexandria, VA: Association for Supervision and Curriculum Development.

Kim, H. (2003, April). *Factors of forming teachers' intention to use the internet in class.* Paper presented at the meeting of the American Educational Research Association, Chicago, IL.

Kowalski, T. J. (2003). *Contemporary school administration: An introduction.* Boston: Allyn & Bacon.

LaFee, S. (2002, December). Data-driven districts: Four districts that take different tacks using data to inform key decisions. *The School Administrator Web Edition.* Retrieved June 11, 2004, from http://www.aasa.org/publications/sa/2002_12/LaFee.htm.

Lewin, K. (1951). *Field theory in social science.* New York: Harper & Row.

Patton, M. Q. (1978). *Utilization-focused evaluation.* Beverly Hills, CA: Sage.

Peterson, K. D. (2002). Positive or negative? *Journal of Staff Development, 23*(3), 10–15.

Pryor, B. W. (1990). Predicting and explaining intentions to participate in continuing education: An application of the theory of reasoned action. *Adult Education Quarterly, 40,* 146–157.

Pryor, C. R., & Kang, R. (2003). Two new evaluation instruments for collaboration. *Academic Exchange Quarterly, 7*(3), 147–151.

Shepard, G. J. (1987). Individual differences in the relationship between attitudinal and normative determinants of behavioral intent. *Communication Monographs, 54,* 221–231.

Thacker, J. L., & McInerney, W. D. (1992). Changing academic culture to improve student achievement in elementary schools. *ERS Spectrum, 10*(4), 18–23.

Thompson, S. (Ed.). (2001). The school leadership challenge. *Strategies, 8*(1), 1–16.

Thornburg, G. E., & Pryor, B. W. (1998). Attitudinal and normative predictors of continuing library education: An application of the theory of reasoned action. *Journal of Education for Library and Information Science, 39*(2), 118–133.

Waugh, R. G., & Punch, K. F. (1987). Teacher receptivity to system-wide change in the implementation stage. *Review of Educational Research, 57*(3), 237–254.

Welch, M. (1989). A cultural perspective and the second wave of educational reform. *Journal of Learning Disabilities, 22*(9), 537–540, 560.

Index

Administrators, 3, 11–12, 15, 99, 108. *See also* Principals
Ajzen, I., 75
Analysis. *See* Data analysis
ANOVA tests, 91
Attitudes:
  behavioral intention and. *See* Behavioral intention, attitude and
  beliefs and, 23–25, 27. *See also* Beliefs
  case studies about, 25–32, 39–43
  changing, 25–26, 28–33, 38–43, 57, 102–106
  defined, 21, 22, 35, 111
  examples of, 26–27, 36
  formation of, 12, 22–25 (figure), 26–29, 33, 36–39 (figure), 100, 102
  global, 2, 36
  group, 11, 13
  levels of, 22, 36
  measuring. *See* Data collection, measuring attitudes for
  outcomes and. *See* Beliefs, outcomes and
  relative importance of, 46, 55–56, 59, 88, 100
  research on, 46
  scales measuring, 23, 113–114
  specific, 22, 36
  strength of, 35
  student, 11
  teacher, 10, 25–27
  toward behaviors, 35–43, 58
  toward objects and people, 22–33
  See also Beliefs; Norms

Behavioral categories, 65, 67. *See also* Behaviors
Behavioral intention:
  attitude and, 4 (figure), 5–7, 10–11
  changing, 5
  defined, 111
  formation of, 4 (figure), 5, 88
  personal and social factors and, 4, 55
  relative influence of attitude and norm in, 5–6
  scale, 114
  subjective norm and, 4 (figure), 5–7. *See also* Norms
  See also Behaviors
Behaviors:
  attitudes toward. *See* Attitudes, toward behaviors
  changing, 5–6
  context of, 66, 67
  defined, 111
  making decisions about, 3–4
  outcomes of, 58, 66, 67
  planned, 6–7
  research on, 6
  single, 65
  target of, 67
  time of, 66–67
  See also Behavioral categories; Behavioral intention

Belief structures, 3, 5.
    See also Beliefs
Beliefs:
    acceptance of information and, 8
    acquiring, 7–8
    adding new, 31–32, 43, 105
    attitudes and, 23–25, 27.
        See also Attitudes
    belief sets and, 88–89
    changing, 106
    data analysis on.
        See Data analysis
    data collection on.
        See Data collection
    defined, 111
    direct observation and, 8
    duration of, 37
    eliciting, 70–72.
        See also Data collection
    evaluation of, 23–24, 28–32,
        37–38, 56–57, 101, 102, 114
    evaluation products, 102, 106
    examples of, 27–28
    measuring, 77–79.
        See also Data collection
    normative, 46–47, 56, 58, 71, 77,
        106, 107 (table), 108, 115.
        See also Norms
    outcomes and, 36–43, 56–57,
        71–72, 100–106, 114
    planned behaviors and, 6–7
    qualities of an object and,
        22–24
    relative importance of, 8–9
    salient, 8–9, 22, 28, 32, 36, 70,
        72–77
    scale, 114
    school culture and, 25
    strength of, 37, 58,
        102–104, 108
    See also Attitudes; Belief
        structures; Norms
Brainstorming, 12–13

Case studies:
    attitude, 25–32, 39–43
    norms, 49–53

overview of, 18–19
    teacher retention, 99–109
Concerns-Based Adoption Model
    (CBAM), 10

Darling-Hammond, Linda,
    3, 5, 6, 7
Data analysis
    beta weights and, 87, 88, 100
    correlation and, 86–89
    data entry for, 85
    differences between intention
        groups in, 89–93 (table),
        94 (table), 95 (table), 101
        (table), 107 (table)
    frequency distributions in,
        89, 90 (table)
    influence of beliefs underlying
        norms in, 96–98
    linear relationships in, 86
    relative influence of attitude
        and norm in, 88, 100
    reporting results of,
        85, 93–95, 98
    statistical procedures
        used for, 86–87
    statistical significance in,
        87, 91–92, 101
    testing in-common
        belief sets in, 88–89
    transforming scores
        on scales for, 86
    using multiple regression in,
        88, 100
    valid and cumulative percents
        in, 90
    value scale in, 89
    See also Data collection
Data collection:
    adding variables for, 79–80
    background information for, 79
    deciding how many beliefs
        to include for, 75–77
    effective, 81
    eliciting outcome and normative
        beliefs for, 69–77
    evaluative scales for, 78

grouping related beliefs
    for, 74–75
identification of common
    beliefs for, 75–76 (table)
interviews, 70–72
measuring attitudes for, 78–79
measuring beliefs for, 77–79
measuring subjective
    norms for, 78–79
organizing data for, 72–74
    (table), 75–77
probability scales for, 78–79
questionnaires, 70–72, 80,
    117–125
questions, 71
selecting salient beliefs
    for, 72–77
selecting samples for, 69–70
social desirability bias and, 71
steps for, 69, 81
See also Data analysis
Decision-making, 12, 15
Dillman, Don, 81

Evaluation. *See* Beliefs,
    evaluation of

Fishbein, M., 75
Force field analysis, 12–13
Fullan, Michael, 11

Glossary of key terms, 111
Goodlad, John, 11
Group decision making, 13
Guilford Self-Rating Scale, 113

Have You Got Attitude?:
    Understanding and Changing
    Motivation and Behavior, 111
Hord, Shirley, 12

Intention. *See* Behavioral intention

Lewin, Kurt, 12

Mail and Internet Surveys: The
    'Tailored Design Method, 81

Model of Reasoned
    Action (MORA):
abbreviated use of, 14
administrator use of, 15.
    See also Administrators
advantages of, 10–17, 99
attitudes and. *See* Attitudes
beliefs and. *See* Beliefs
case studies about.
    See Case studies
checklist for, 127–129
decision making and, 13, 55–56
district level use of, 15–16
emotion and, 17
ethics of, 16
examples of, 17–20, 56–57, 97,
    99–109. *See also* Case studies
figure of, 56
hypothetical results from
    applying, 97 (figure)
implications for school
    leaders of, 3
internet-based resources for,
    131–132
irrational people and, 17
norms and. *See* Norms
personal and social factors
    and, 4, 55
population of interest for,
    64–65, 67, 69–70
research on, 6
researchable questions
    for, 63–67
school culture and, 9, 25
school level use of, 16
specific groups and, 10
statistical procedures for.
    See Data analysis
uses of, 3, 12, 13–14, 14–20
See also Attitudes; Beliefs; Norms
Motivation. *See* Norms,
    motivation to comply with

Norms:
case study about, 49–53
change of, 48–49, 50–53,
    58, 106, 108–109

defined, 45, 111
formation of, 46–51 (figure),
    57, 106
measuring, 47–48, 78–79
motivation to comply with,
    47–48, 56, 57–58, 107, 115
normative beliefs and, 46–49, 58.
    See also Beliefs, normative
normative pressure and, 52
referents and, 46–53, 57–58,
    108–109
relative importance of, 46,
    55–56, 59, 88, 100
research on, 46, 48
scales of, 115
subjective, 45–46, 48–49
    (figure), 52 (figure),
    57–58, 100, 106, 111, 115
See also Attitudes; Beliefs

Parents, 64, 108
Patton, Michael Quinn, 80
Pearson's product moment
    correlation, 86, 88–89
Peterson, Kent, 9
Principals:
    as referents, 108
    expectations of, 47
    problems of, 10, 99
    using MORA to retain teachers,
        99–109
    See also Administrators;
        Case studies
Punch, K. F., 10

Questionnaire, sample, 117–125.
    See also Data collection
    questionnaires

Referents. *See* Norms,
    referents and

Scales, sample, 113–115
School change, 10–12, 63
School concerns, 63
School culture, 9, 25
Semantic Differential Scale, 114
*Statistical Package for the
    Social Sciences* (SPSS),
    85, 86, 89, 90
Statistical procedures.
    See Data analysis, statistical
    procedures used for
Students, 11, 47, 104, 108

Teacher Assistance
    Program (TAP), 103
Teachers:
    attitudes of, 10, 25–27
    motivations of, 47
    retention of, 99–109.
        See also Case studies
    using MORA with, 14–15, 64
Thompson, S., 10

Voters, 64

Waugh, R.G., 10
Welch, M., 10

**CORWIN
PRESS**

The Corwin Press logo—a raven striding across an open book—
represents the union of courage and learning. Corwin Press is
committed to improving education for all learners by publishing
books and other professional development resources for those
serving the field of K–12 education. By providing practical, hands-on
materials, Corwin Press continues to carry out the promise of its
motto: **"Helping Educators Do Their Work Better."**